Pattern+Palette
SOURCEBOOK

ROCKPORT

First published in the United States of America by
Rockport Publishers, Inc.
33 Commercial Street
Gloucester, Massachusetts 01930-5089
Telephone: 978.282.9590
Fax: 978.283.2742
www.rockpub.com

ISBN 1-59253-161-X

10 9 8 7 6 5 4 3 2 1

Design: Anvil Graphic Design, Inc.
CD-ROM production: SYP Design & Production, Inc., www.sypdesign.com
Grateful acknowledgment is given to Anvil Graphic Design, Inc. whose original patterns appear
on pages 6–73 and 176–207.

Patterns appearing on pages 75–175 were printed previously in *Color Sourcebook* (Rockport Publishers, 1989)
and *Color Sourcebook II* (Rockport Publishers, 1989).

Printed in Singapore

Pattern + Palette

SOURCEBOOK

A Complete Guide to Choosing the
Perfect Color and Pattern in Design

GLOUCESTER MASSACHUSETTS

ROCKPORT PUBLISHERS

Compiled by
Anvil Graphic Design, Inc.

Contents

Pattern and Palette Sourcebook is a comprehensive guide to color coordination and balance in pattern, providing a practical insight into the nature and application of color combination. Because color is such an intimate part of everyday life, we never think twice about describing colors as being "somber," "festive," "cold," "loud," or "friendly." What this means is that no color exists for us in isolation. Without a frame of reference, usually other related colors, any color is essentially meaningless.

This manual is based on the concept that color harmonies and discords are culturally directed, and that by thinking in terms of cultural criteria the designer can get a head start in effective color design. The color and pattern combinations are arranged here under the headings Fashion, Pop, Deco, Asian, Natural, and Industrial, creating a framework for trends in color and pattern.

Each page presents five examples of patterns that were developed using two or more of the color samples at the top of the page. By studying and experimenting with these patterns, you can see how any two or more colors work together to create different effects. The same coordinated set of colors can say vastly different things, depending on how they are assembled and applied. Use these applications as a "casebook" to help you arrive at effective color schemes more quickly, accurately, and creatively.

These colors take their cue from the fashion trends of today. From the haute couture creations on the runway to the glossy pages of the fashion magazines, this palette, combined with graphic and often retro modern patterns, adds a level of sophistication to any context.

Fashion

C	0	11	45	0	0	0
M	45	0	0	75	25	2
Y	91	66	9	75	45	87
K	0	2	0	0	40	59

1

2

3

4

5

C	0	0	35
M	45	3	9
Y	91	87	0
K	0	30	0

0	0	0	
36	53	0	
14	100	0	
0	72	100	

6

7

8

9

10

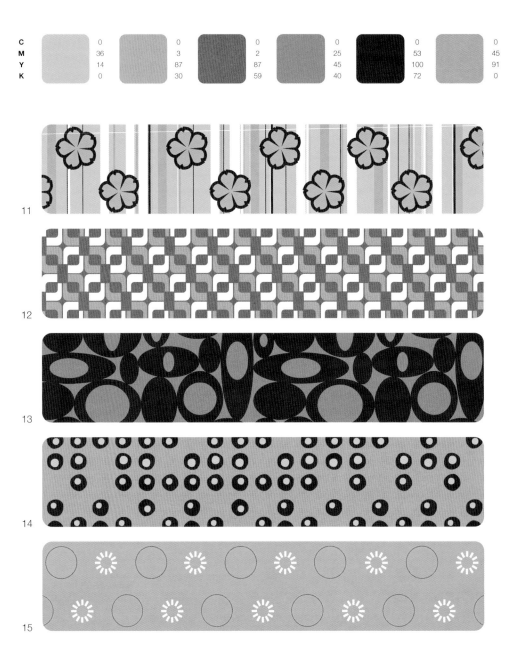

C	0		0		0		0		0		0
M	36		3		2		25		53		45
Y	14		87		87		45		100		91
K	0		30		59		40		72		0

11

12

13

14

15

C	0		0		45		0
M	45		75		0		75
Y	91		15		9		75
K	0		15		0		0

16

17

18

19

20

	C									
C		0		0		0		11		0		100

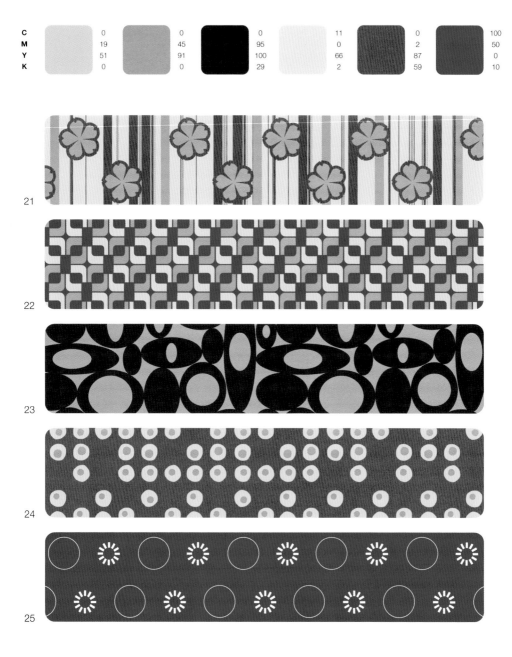

C		0		0		0		11		0		100
M		19		45		95		0		2		50
Y		51		91		100		66		87		0
K		0		0		29		2		59		10

21

22

23

24

25

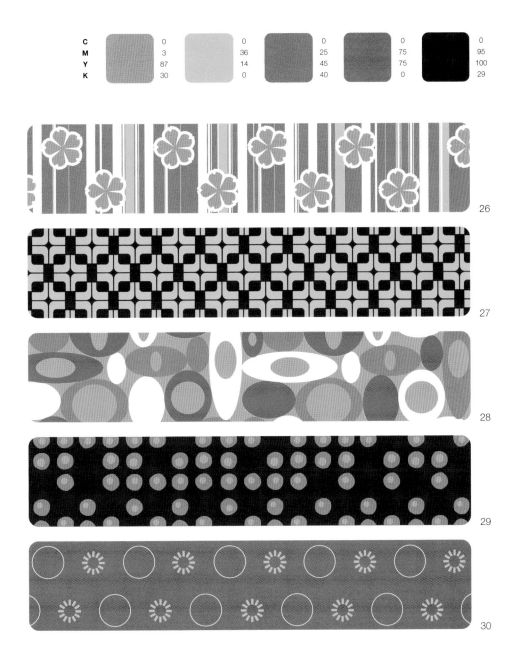

C	0	0	0	0	0
M	3	36	25	75	95
Y	87	14	45	75	100
K	30	0	40	0	29

26

27

28

29

30

C	0		0		35		0		0		0
M	19		36		9		95		75		0
Y	51		14		0		100		15		0
K	0		0		0		29		15		100

31

32

33

34

35

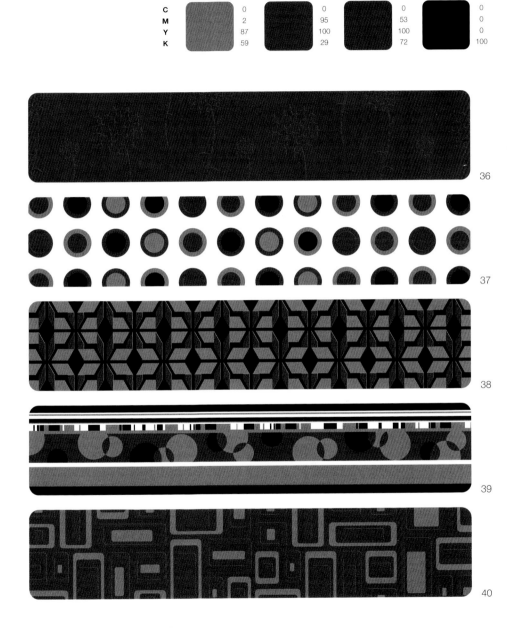

C	0	0	0	0
M	2	95	53	0
Y	87	100	100	0
K	59	29	72	100

36

37

38

39

40

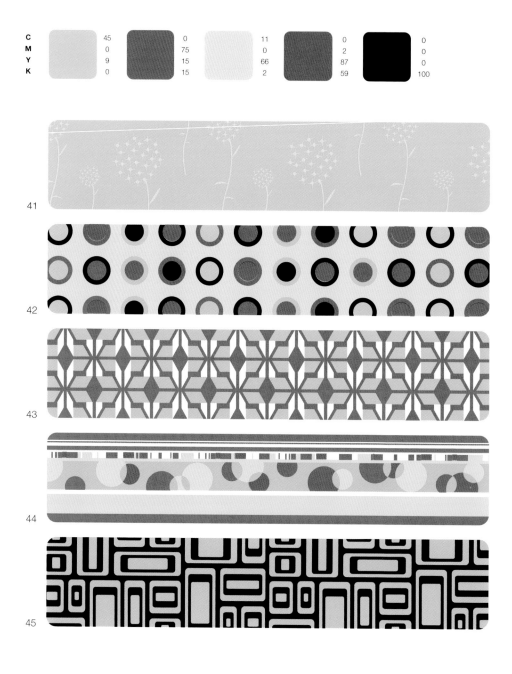

C	45	0	11	0	0
M	0	75	0	2	0
Y	9	15	66	87	0
K	0	15	2	59	100

41

42

43

44

45

C	11	0	35	100	0
M	0	3	9	50	95
Y	66	87	0	0	100
K	2	30	0	10	29

46

47

48

49

50

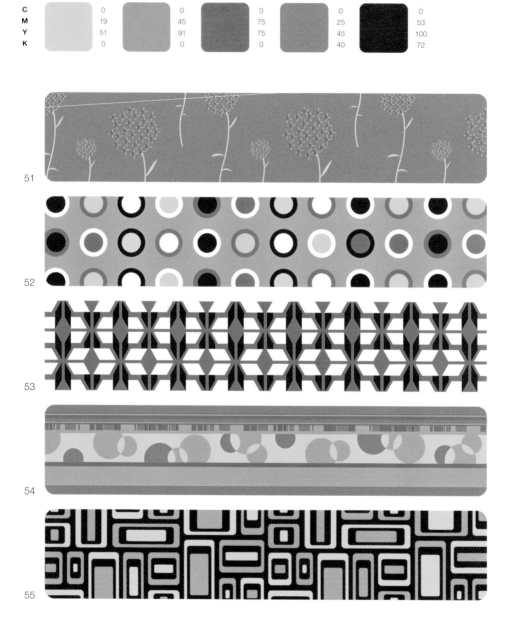

C	0	0	0	0	0
M	19	45	75	25	53
Y	51	91	75	45	100
K	0	0	0	40	72

51

52

53

54

55

C		0		35		11		0
M		36		9		0		25
Y		14		0		66		45
K		0		0		2		40

56

57

58

59

60

C			0		0		0		45		11		0
M			25		75		45		0		0		2
Y			45		75		91		9		66		87
K			40		0		0		0		2		59

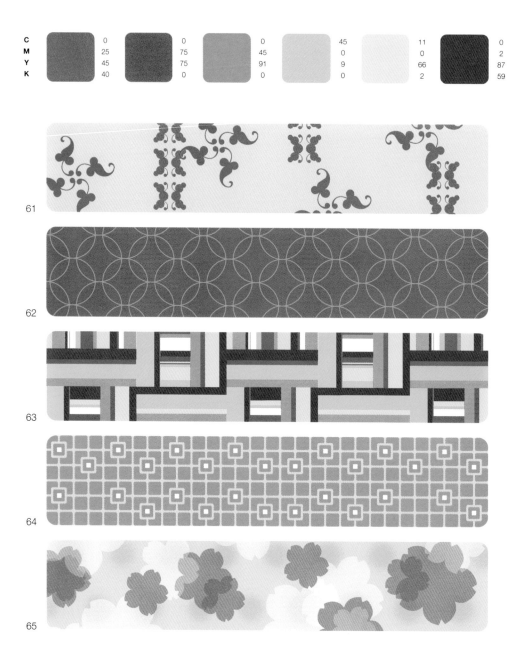

61

62

63

64

65

C	0		0		0		100		0
M	75		25		3		50		0
Y	15		45		87		0		0
K	15		40		30		10		100

66

67

68

69

70

		45		0		0		0
C		45		0		0		0
M		0		75		45		75
Y		9		75		91		15
K		0		0		0		15

71

72

73

74

75

C		11		0		100		0		0		0
M		0		19		50		45		95		2
Y		66		51		0		91		100		87
K		2		0		10		0		29		59

76

77

78

79

80

C		0		0		0		0		35		0
M		0		53		45		36		9		3
Y		0		100		91		14		0		87
K		100		72		0		0		0		30

81

82

83

84

85

C	35	11	0	0	100
M	9	0	75	53	50
Y	0	66	75	100	0
K	0	2	0	72	10

86

87

88

89

90

C	0		0		0		45		11
M	2		75		0		0		0
Y	87		15		0		9		66
K	59		15		100		0		2

91

92

93

94

95

C	0	0	0	0	0
M	45	25	19	53	75
Y	91	45	51	100	75
K	0	40	0	72	0

96

97

98

99

100

C	0		0		35		0		0		0
M	95		0		9		75		19		36
Y	100		0		0		15		51		14
K	29		100		0		15		0		0

101

102

103

104

105

C	0	0	35	45	100
M	19	45	9	0	50
Y	51	91	0	9	0
K	0	0	0	0	10

106

107

108

109

110

C	0		0		0		0			
M	53		2		0		95			
Y	100		87		0		100			
K	72		59		100		29			

111

112

113

114

115

C	35		0		0		11
M	9		25		36		0
Y	0		45		14		66
K	0		40		0		2

116

117

118

119

120

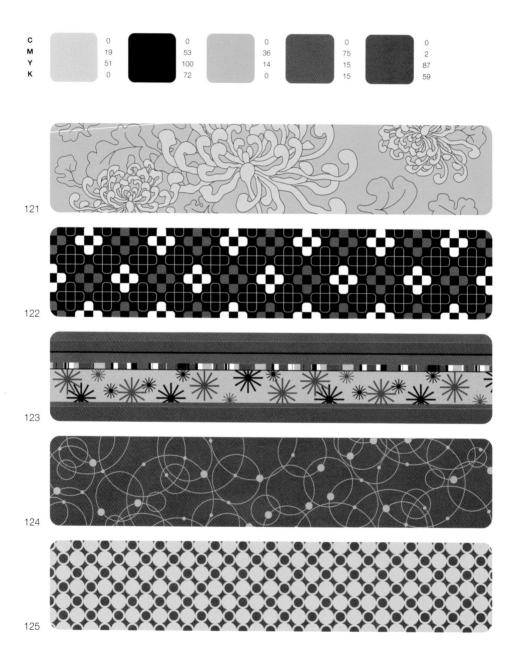

C	0		0		0		0		0
M	19		53		36		75		2
Y	51		100		14		15		87
K	0		72		0		15		59

121

122

123

124

125

C	0		0		0		0		0
M	36		75		3		95		25
Y	14		75		87		100		45
K	0		0		30		29		40

126

127

128

129

130

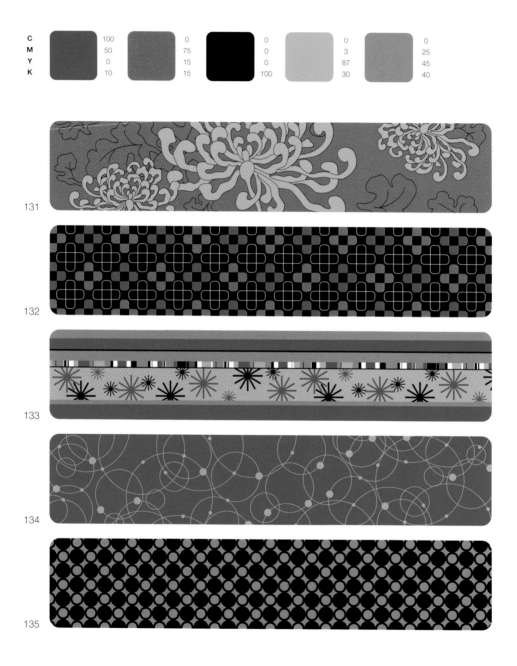

C	100		0		0		0		0
M	50		75		0		3		25
Y	0		15		0		87		45
K	10		15		100		30		40

131

132

133

134

135

C 0	**C** 0	**C** 0	**C** 0	**C** 0
M 36	**M** 2	**M** 19	**M** 75	**M** 53
Y 14	**Y** 87	**Y** 51	**Y** 15	**Y** 100
K 0	**K** 59	**K** 0	**K** 15	**K** 72

136

137

138

139

140

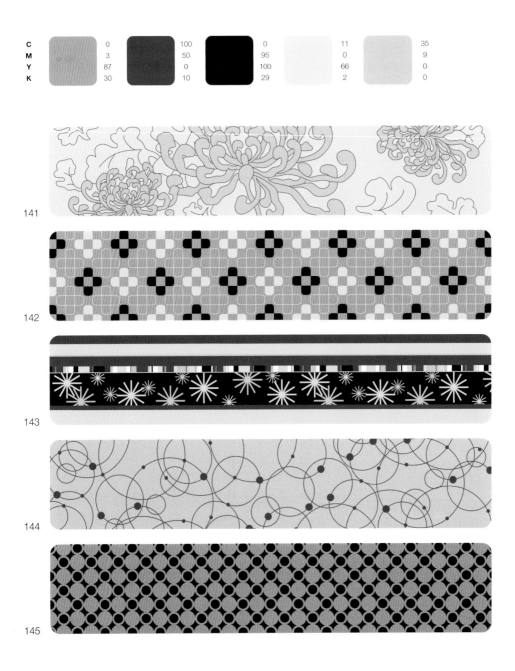

C		0		100		0		11		35
M		3		50		95		0		9
Y		87		0		100		66		0
K		30		10		29		2		0

141

142

143

144

145

C	0		0		0		0		0		0
M	53		3		36		25		45		2
Y	100		87		14		45		91		87
K	72		30		0		40		0		59

146

147

148

149

150

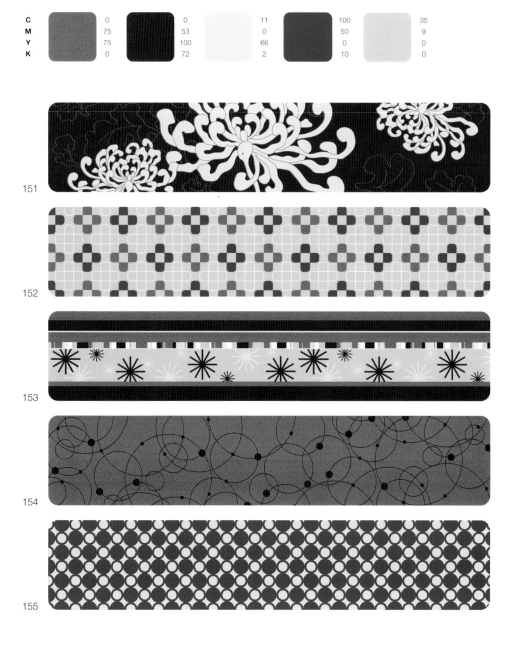

C	0		0		11		100		35
M	75		53		0		50		9
Y	75		100		66		0		0
K	0		72		2		10		0

151

152

153

154

155

C	100	35	0	45	0
M	50	9	19	0	45
Y	0	0	51	9	91
K	10	0	0	0	0

156

157

158

159

160

This bright and primary palette can create a myriad of electric color combinations. Paired with patterns reminiscent of the groovy era of the '60s—from Andy Warhol-esque pop art to optical illusions—any composition can take on a vibrant, or even psychedelic, personality.

Pop

C		40		100		40		100		0		0
M		0		0		0		0		0		100
Y		10		0		90		100		90		100
K		0		0		0		0		0		0

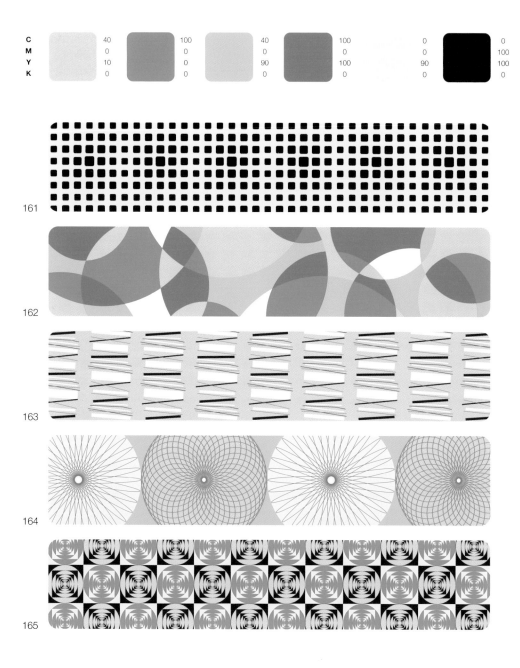

161

162

163

164

165

C		0		0		90		20		0
M		0		40		60		20		0
Y		0		100		0		0		0
K		20		0		0		0		75

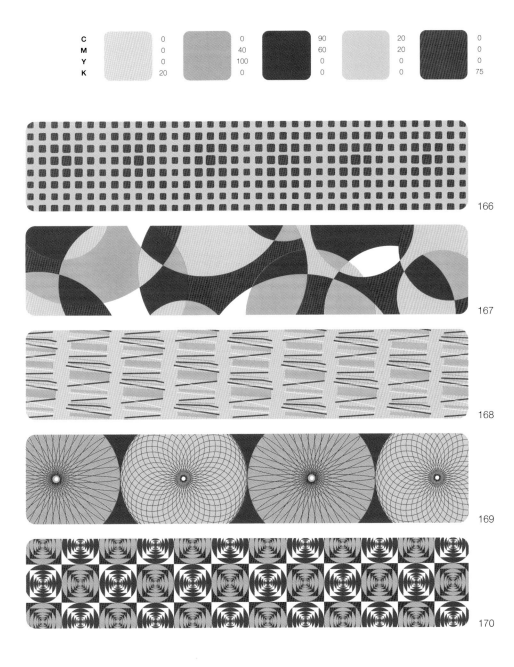

166

167

168

169

170

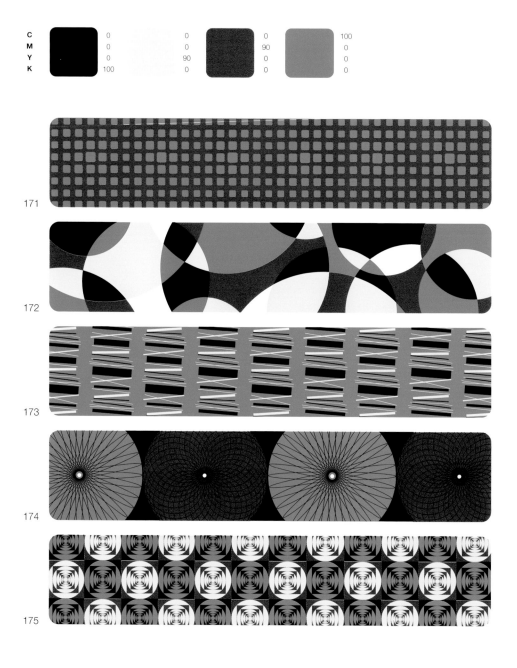

C		0		0		0		100
M		0		0		90		0
Y		0		90		0		0
K		100		0		0		0

171

172

173

174

175

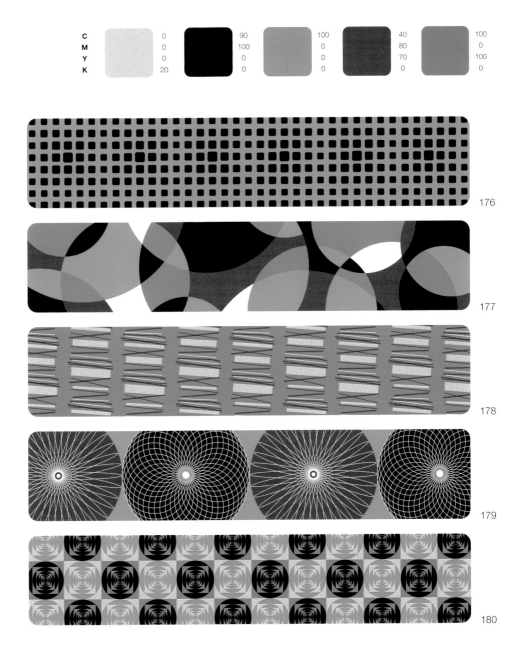

	C	0		90		100		40		100
	M	0		100		0		80		0
	Y	0		0		0		70		100
	K	20		0		0		0		0

176

177

178

179

180

C	0		0		40		40		20		0
M	100		0		0		80		20		0
Y	100		90		10		70		0		0
K	0		0		0		0		0		100

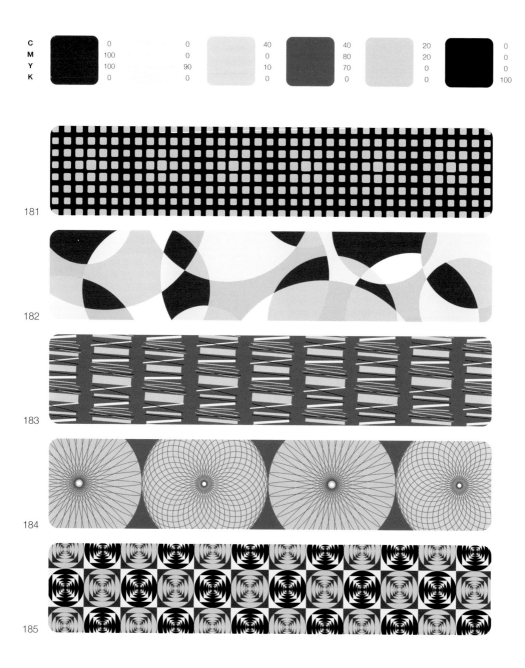

181

182

183

184

185

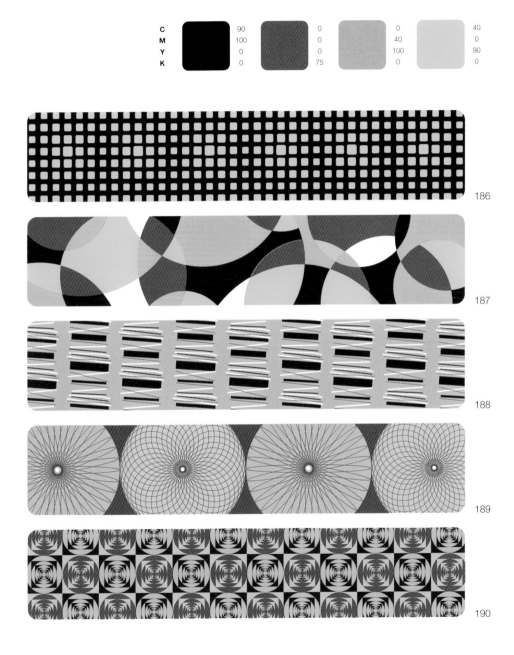

C	90		0		0		40
M	100		0		40		0
Y	0		0		100		90
K	0		75		0		0

186

187

188

189

190

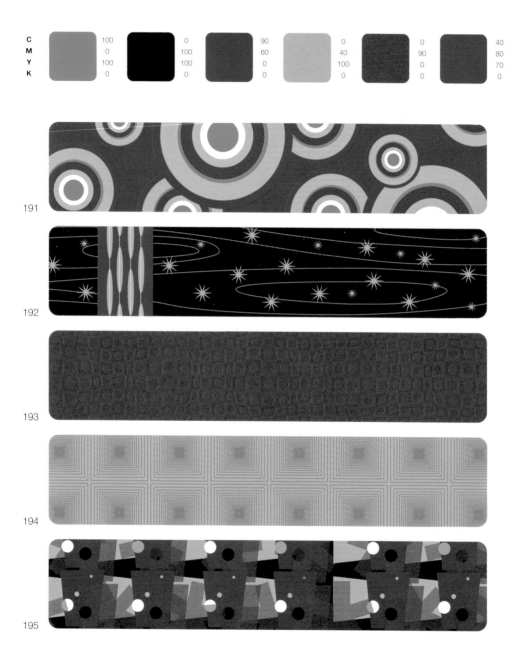

C	100		0		90		0		0		40
M	0		100		60		40		90		80
Y	100		100		0		100		0		70
K	0		0		0		0		0		0

191

192

193

194

195

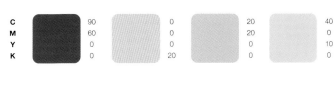

C	90		0		20		40
M	60		0		20		0
Y	0		0		20		10
K	0		20		0		0

196

197

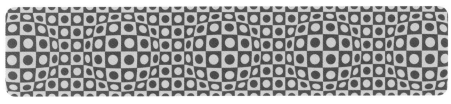

198

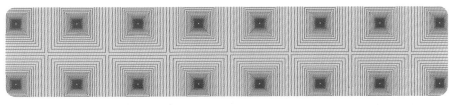

199

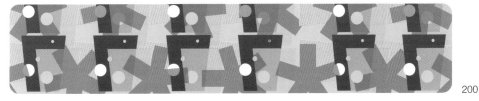

200

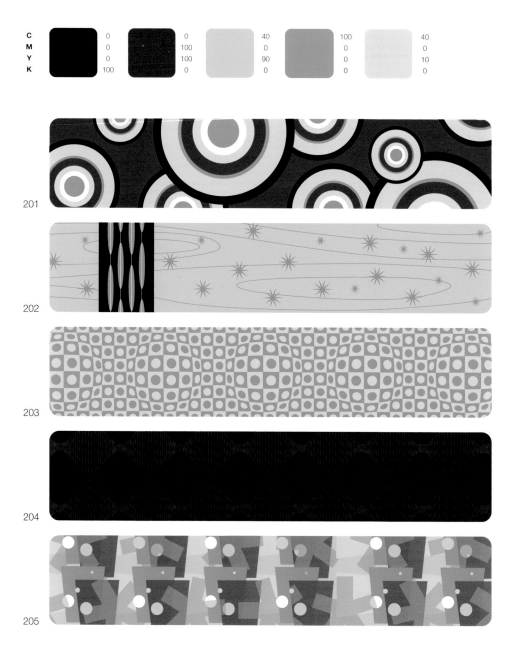

C	0		0		40		100		40
M	0		100		0		0		0
Y	0		100		90		0		10
K	100		0		0		0		0

201

202

203

204

205

C		40		90		0		0		90
M		0		60		0		90		100
Y		90		0		90		0		0
K		0		0		0		0		0

206

207

208

209

210

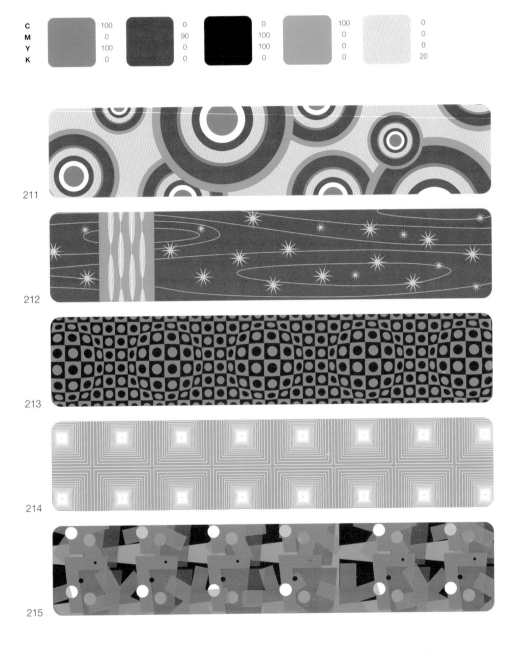

C	100	0	0	100	0
M	0	90	100	0	0
Y	100	0	100	0	0
K	0	0	0	0	20

211

212

213

214

215

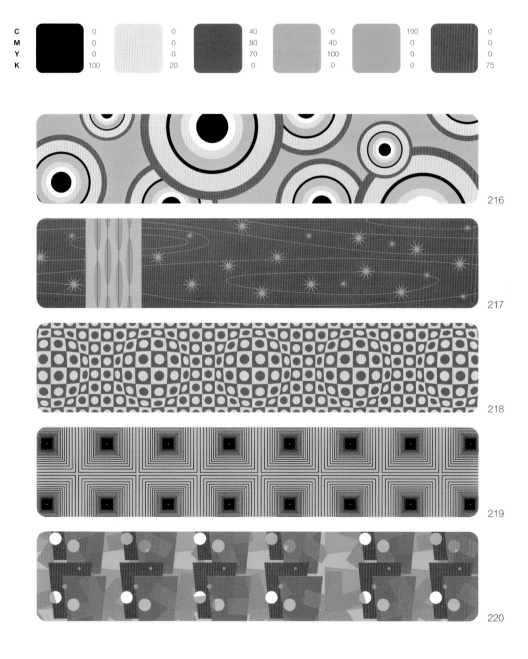

	C	M	Y	K
	0	0	0	100
	0	0	0	20
	40	80	70	0
	0	40	100	0
	100	0	0	0
	0	0	0	75

216

217

218

219

220

C		0		0		0		0		20		90
M		0		0		90		0		20		100
Y		0		0		0		0		0		0
K		100		20		0		75		0		0

221

222

223

224

225

C	100		0		0		100		40		40
M	0		0		100		0		0		0
Y	100		90		100		0		90		10
K	0		0		0		0		0		0

226

227

228

229

230

C	90	0	100	0	0
M	60	0	0	90	0
Y	0	0	90	0	0
K	0	0	0	0	100

231

232

233

234

235

C		0		0		0		20		90
M		40		0		100		20		100
Y		100		90		100		0		0
K		0		0		0		0		0

236

237

238

239

240

C	40		40		0		0		100
M	0		0		100		0		0
Y	90		10		100		0		0
K	0		0		0		100		0

241

242

243

244

245

C	0		90		40		0
M	40		100		0		0
Y	100		0		90		0
K	0		0		0		75

246

247

248

249

250

C	100		0		0		0		90
M	0		0		0		90		60
Y	100		0		90		0		0
K	0		100		0		0		0

251

252

253

254

255

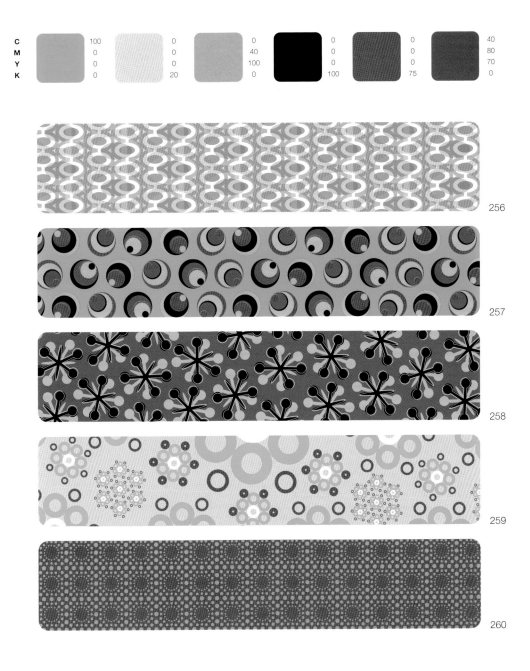

C	100		0		0		0		0		40
M	0		0		40		0		0		80
Y	0		0		100		0		0		70
K	0		20		0		100		75		0

256

257

258

259

260

C	0	90	0	0	20
M	100	100	0	40	20
Y	100	0	90	100	0
K	0	0	0	0	0

261

262

263

264

265

C	M	Y	K
0	0	0	75
40	0	90	0
40	0	10	0
0	40	100	0
40	80	70	0

266

267

268

269

270

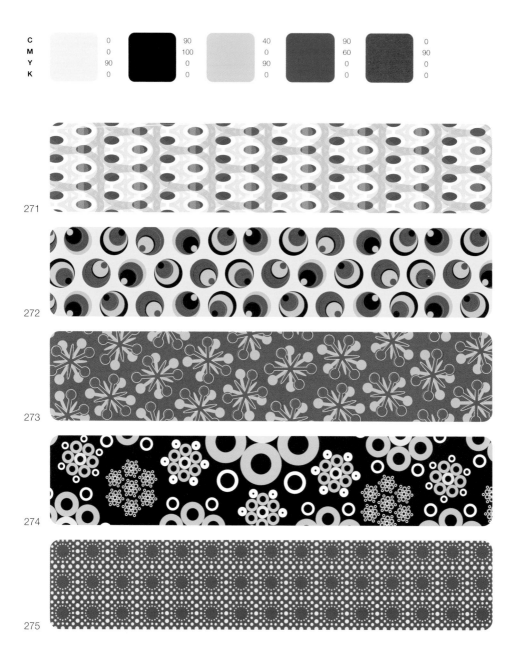

C	0	90	40	90	0
M	0	100	0	60	90
Y	90	0	90	0	0
K	0	0	0	0	0

271

272

273

274

275

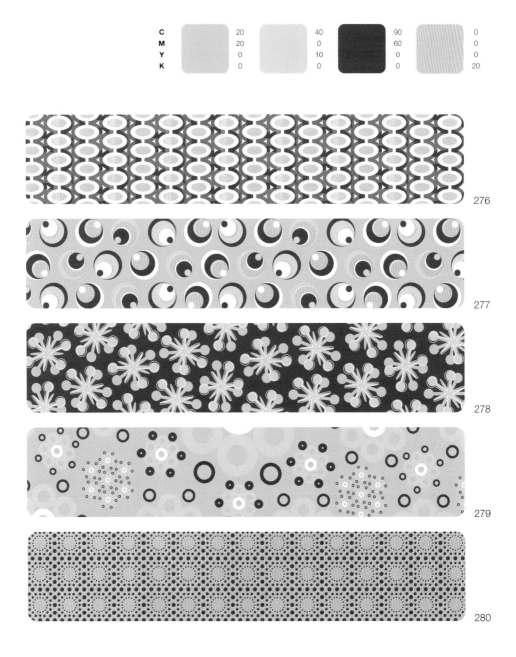

C		20		40		90		0
M		20		0		60		0
Y		0		10		0		0
K		0		0		0		20

276

277

278

279

280

C	0	100	100	0	0
M	100	0	0	81	0
Y	100	0	100	0	0
K	0	0	0	0	20

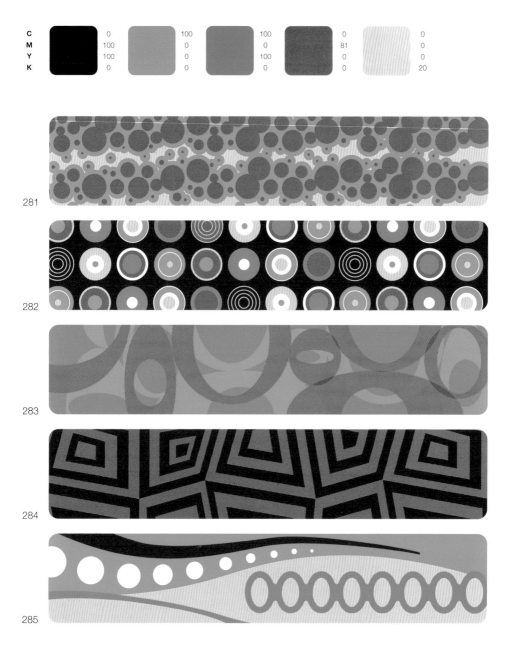

281

282

283

284

285

C	40		0		0		20		0		40
M	0		0		0		20		100		80
Y	10		0		90		0		100		70
K	0		100		0		0		0		0

286

287

288

289

290

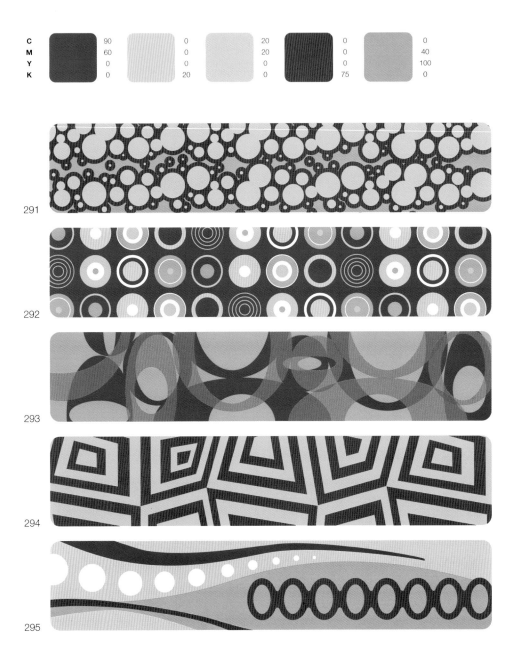

C	90	0	20	0	0
M	60	0	20	0	40
Y	0	0	0	0	100
K	0	20	0	75	0

291

292

293

294

295

C		0		0		100		0		
M		90		0		0		0		
Y		0		0		0		90		
K		0		100		0		0		

296

297

298

299

300

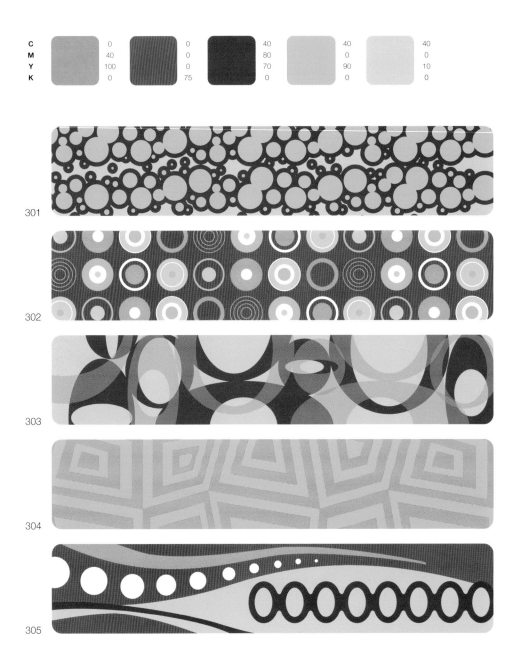

C					
C	0	0	40	40	40
M	40	0	80	0	0
Y	100	0	70	90	10
K	0	75	0	0	0

301

302

303

304

305

C	20	0	0	90	0	0
M	20	90	0	100	0	0
Y	0	0	0	0	0	0
K	0	0	20	0	100	75

306

307

308

309

310

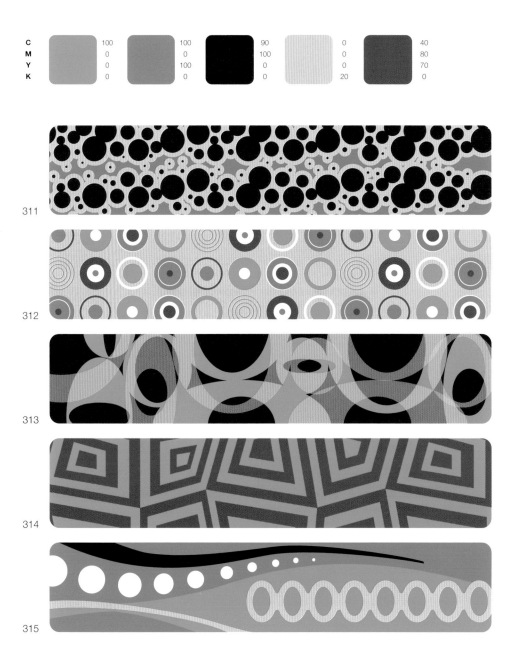

		100		100		90		0		40
C		100		100		90		0		40
M		0		0		100		0		80
Y		0		100		0		0		70
K		0		0		0		20		0

311

312

313

314

315

C	0		90		100		40		0		0
M	90		60		0		80		100		40
Y	0		0		100		70		100		100
K	0		0		0		0		0		0

316

317

318

319

320

This palette combines the soft, dusty hues of the Art Nouveau style with the more vivid colors used in Art Deco design. Used with patterns that can be highly decorative and detailed or more modern and graphic, an atmosphere can be created that is both inviting and comfortable.

Deco

*Note: The color palette above is only a sampling of the color range Deco provides. See the following section for a broader selection of Deco colors.

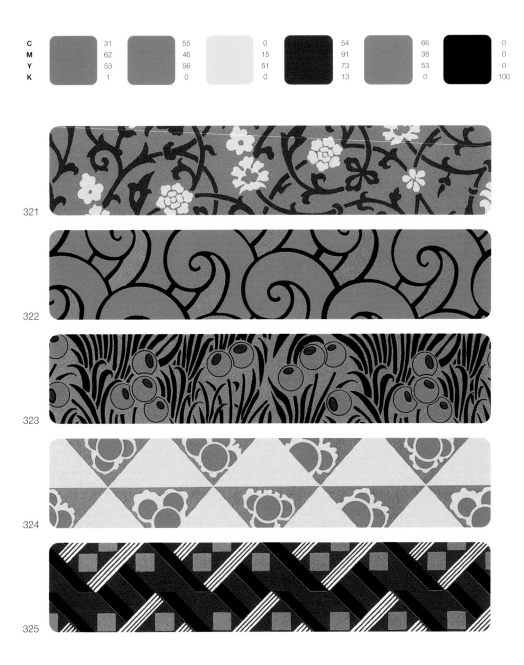

C	31		55		0		54		66		0
M	62		46		15		91		38		0
Y	53		56		51		73		53		0
K	1		0		0		13		0		100

321

322

323

324

325

C	31		0		69		71		56
M	64		35		75		28		51
Y	53		38		94		74		71
K	2		0		20		0		0

326

327

328

329

330

C	31		25		49		81		0
M	60		4		42		76		44
Y	48		25		50		10		62
K	0		0		0		2		0

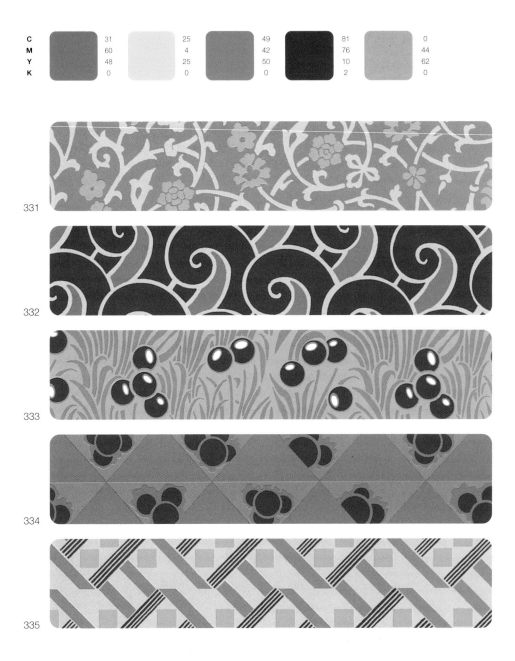

331

332

333

334

335

C	71		13		42		27		11
M	66		53		23		2		22
Y	42		80		25		19		24
K	8		0		0		0		0

336

337

338

339

340

C	61		0		0		9		34
M	62		3		37		25		21
Y	56		38		64		6		58
K	5		0		0		0		0

341

342

343

344

345

C	57		31		45		4		1
M	61		56		42		22		42
Y	44		43		42		30		81
K	2		0		0		0		0

346

347

348

349

350

C						
C	52	54	80	0	93	0
M	45	84	12	20	63	0
Y	75	56	64	34	9	0
K	1	9	0	0	0	100

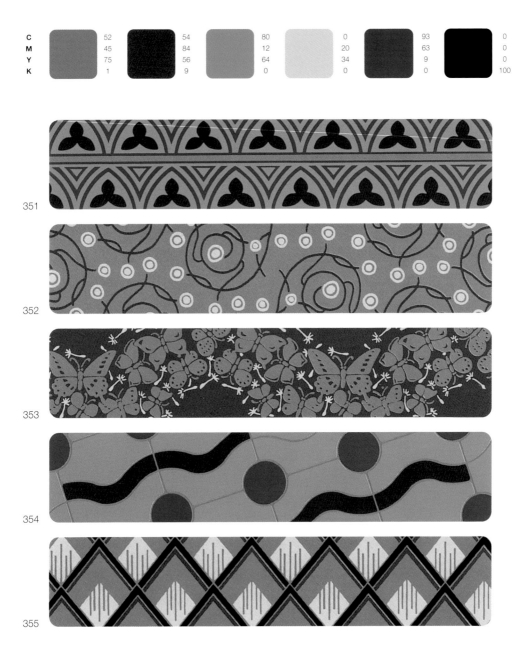

351

352

353

354

355

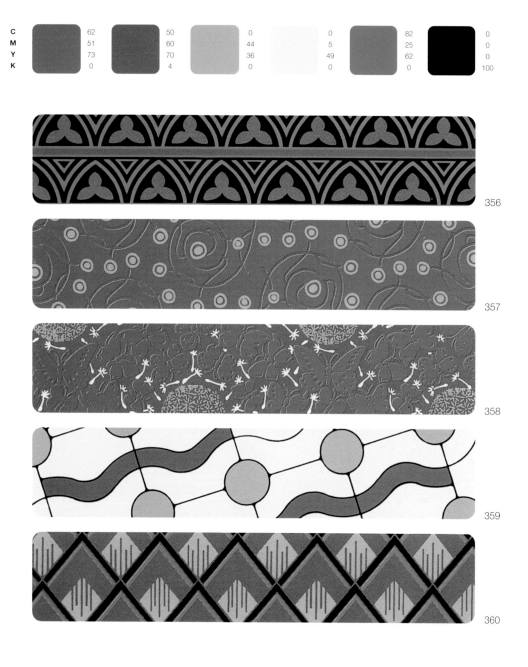

C	62	50	0	0	82	0
M	51	60	44	5	25	0
Y	73	70	36	49	62	0
K	0	4	0	0	0	100

356

357

358

359

360

C	63		38		0		67		23
M	59		30		27		73		92
Y	78		63		24		88		79
K	11		0		0		19		8

361

362

363

364

365

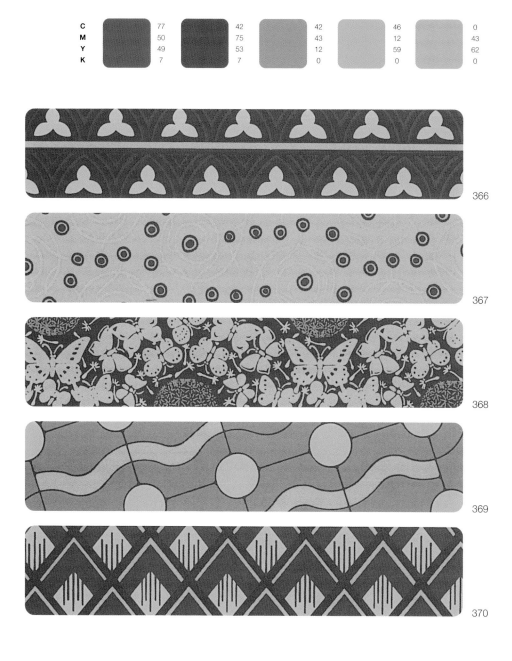

C	77		42		42		46		0
M	50		75		43		12		43
Y	49		53		12		59		62
K	7		7		0		0		0

366

367

368

369

370

C	71	0	64	29	0
M	51	33	68	1	65
Y	47	56	6	18	80
K	4	0	0	0	0

371

372

373

374

375

C	76	73
M	54	84
Y	54	64
K	10	26

	35	13
	47	25
	94	87
	0	0

37
87
77
8

376

377

378

379

380

C	25		65		16		58		97
M	1		51		49		79		97
Y	1		79		68		64		57
K	0		2		0		16		27

381

382

383

384

385

C	23	22	13	72	0
M	1	43	62	66	0
Y	1	95	72	61	0
K	0	0	0	28	100

386

387

388

389

390

C	18	31	62	87	75
M	1	24	37	56	95
Y	1	63	63	45	80
K	0	0	0	7	29

391

392

393

394

395

C	30	9	39	2	73
M	27	43	56	12	85
Y	28	51	73	56	66
K	0	0	0	0	18

396

397

398

399

400

C	17		22		60		56		29
M	11		64		97		58		29
Y	15		97		77		38		54
K	0		0		24		1		0

401

402

403

404

405

C	18		51		69		0		86
M	14		70		55		30		66
Y	10		28		65		43		83
K	0		0		8		0		19

406

407

408

409

410

C	30		68		41		0		40
M	36		85		11		28		77
Y	84		59		45		63		72
K	0		23		0		0		7

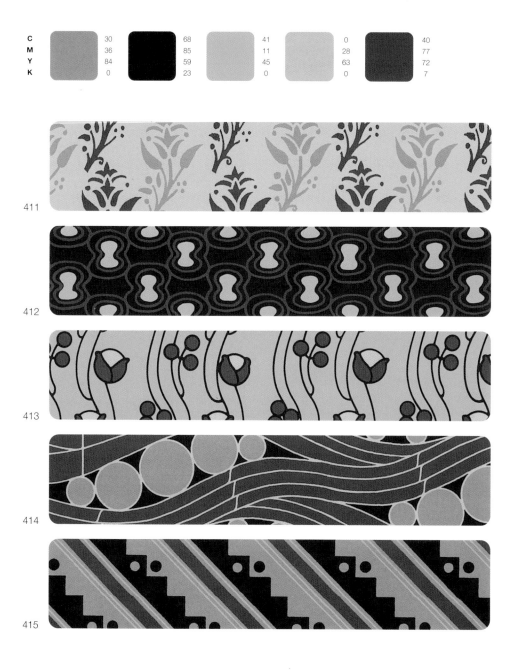

411

412

413

414

415

C		27		97		52		60		49
M		42		85		80		7		56
Y		97		92		76		7		11
K		0		74		14		0		0

416

417

418

419

420

C		38		84		88		1		1
M		43		86		35		30		66
Y		74		42		65		26		87
K		0		11		0		0		0

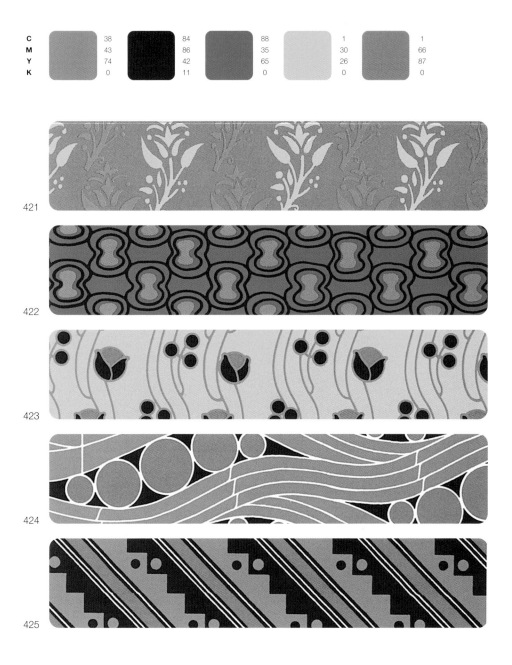

421

422

423

424

425

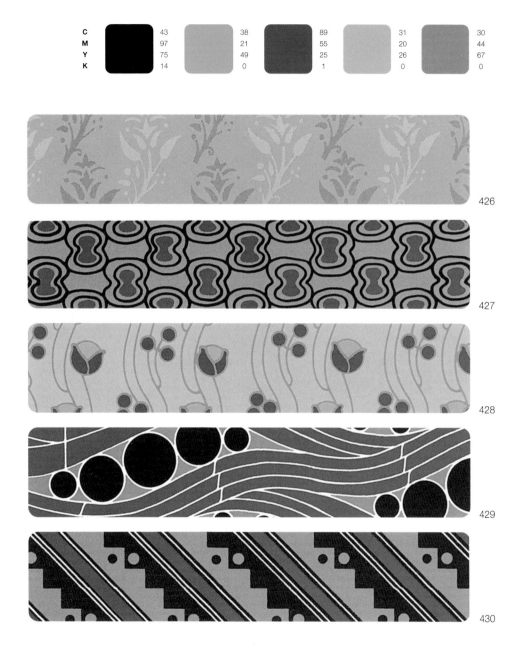

C	43		38		89		31		30
M	97		21		55		20		44
Y	75		49		25		26		67
K	14		0		1		0		0

426

427

428

429

430

C	42		25		71		60		0
M	91		22		69		67		37
Y	86		44		56		42		79
K	13		0		20		3		0

431

432

433

434

435

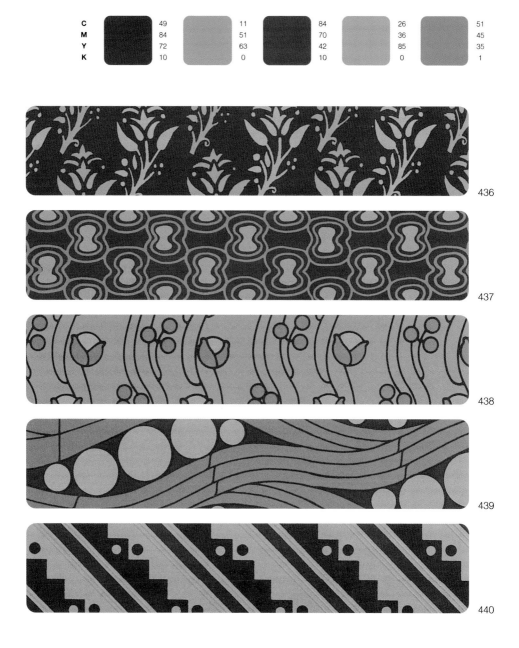

C	49		11		84		26		51
M	84		51		70		36		45
Y	72		63		42		85		35
K	10		0		10		0		1

436

437

438

439

440

C	21	70	46
M	56	80	42
Y	96	40	29
K	0	2	0

45	0
87	0
68	0
9	100

441

442

443

444

445

C 33
M 75
Y 85
K 0

23
0
97
0

46
37
42
0

85
22
74
0

0
0
0
100

446

447

448

449

450

C	29	0	34	·77	0
M	72	15	2	71	0
Y	80	27	2	56	0
K	0	0	0	19	100

451

452

453

454

455

C	77		49		66		0		60
M	75		12		43		24		62
Y	55		62		33		43		69
K	13		0		0		0		13

456

457

458

459

460

C	73		36		40		0		65
M	77		37		73		16		49
Y	62		33		93		58		85
K	12		0		0		0		0

461

462

463

464

465

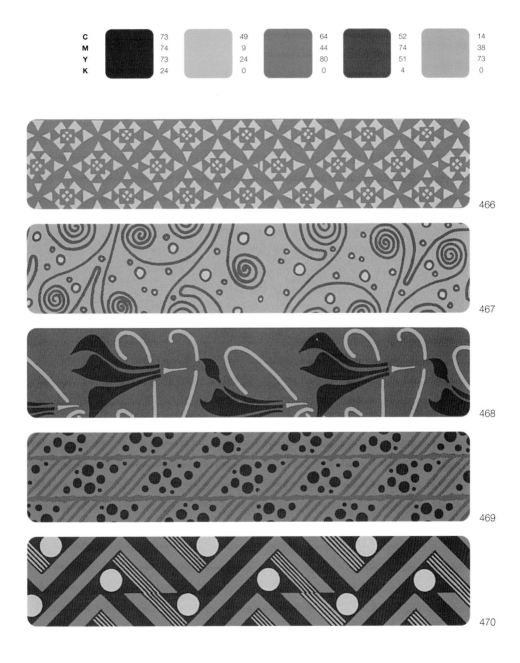

C	73		49		64		52		14
M	74		9		44		74		38
Y	73		24		80		51		73
K	24		0		0		4		0

466

467

468

469

470

C	54		61		26		0		0
M	12		56		40		61		0
Y	65		40		94		79		0
K	0		2		0		0		100

471

472

473

474

475

C	42	84	14	16	10
M	44	89	22	28	75
Y	77	68	59	6	70
K	0	32	0	0	0

476

477

478

479

480

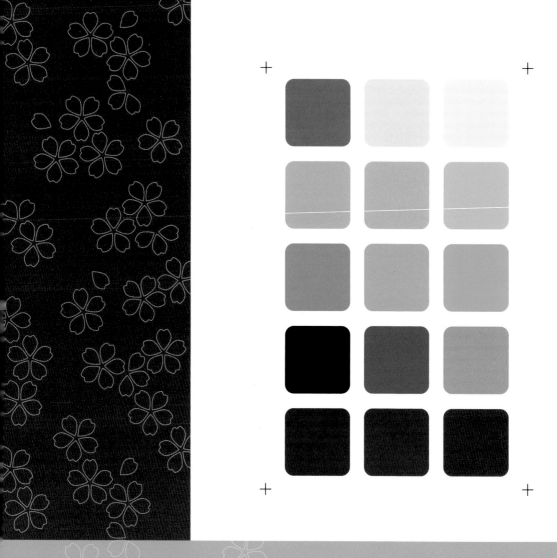

Borrowing from traditional Japanese fabrics and influenced by other Asian motifs, this palette is both dynamic and neutral. The patterns, some of which can be found on kimonos and obis, as well as on decorated papers, inspire a fresh interpretation of traditional design motifs.

Asian

*Note: The color palette above is only a sampling of the color range Asian provides. See the following section for a broader selection of Asian colors.

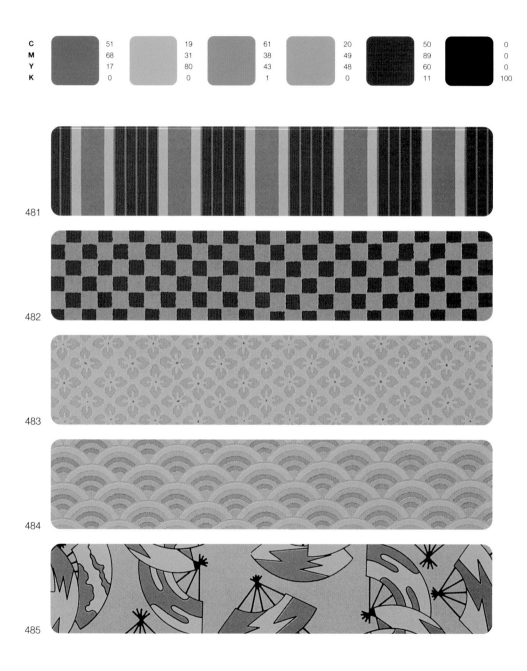

C	51		19		61		20		50		0
M	68		31		38		49		89		0
Y	17		80		43		48		60		0
K	0		0		1		0		11		100

481

482

483

484

485

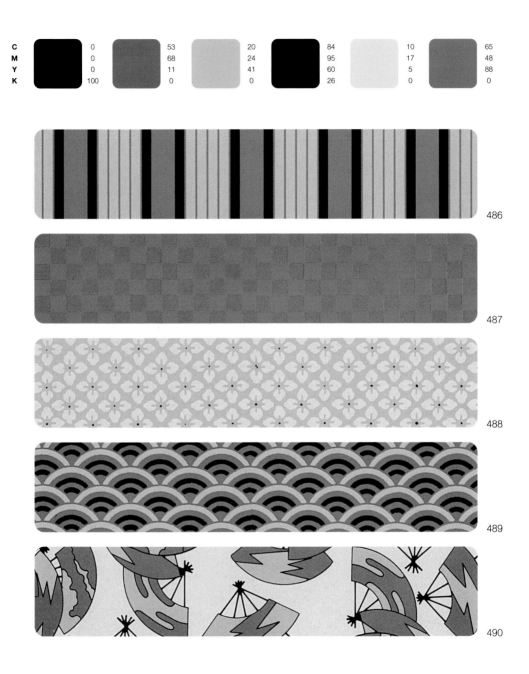

C	0		53		20		84		10		65
M	0		68		24		95		17		48
Y	0		11		41		60		5		88
K	100		0		0		26		0		0

486

487

488

489

490

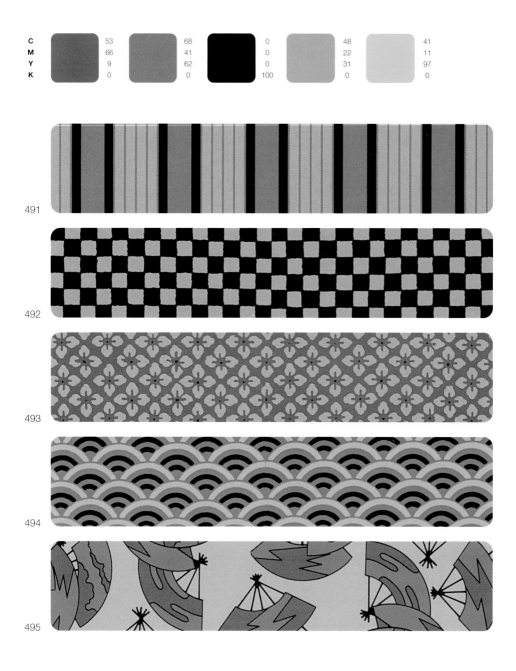

C	53	68	0	48	41
M	66	41	0	22	11
Y	9	62	0	31	97
K	0	0	100	0	0

491

492

493

494

495

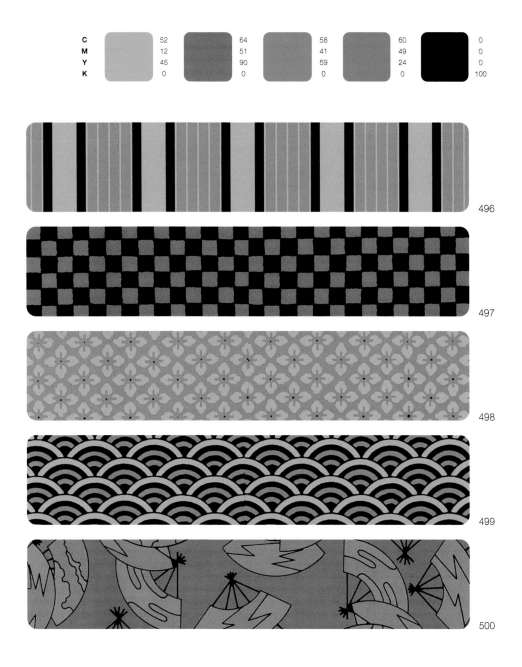

C	52	
M	12	
Y	45	
K	0	

64	
51	
90	
0	

58	
41	
59	
0	

60	
49	
24	
0	

0	
0	
0	
100	

496

497

498

499

500

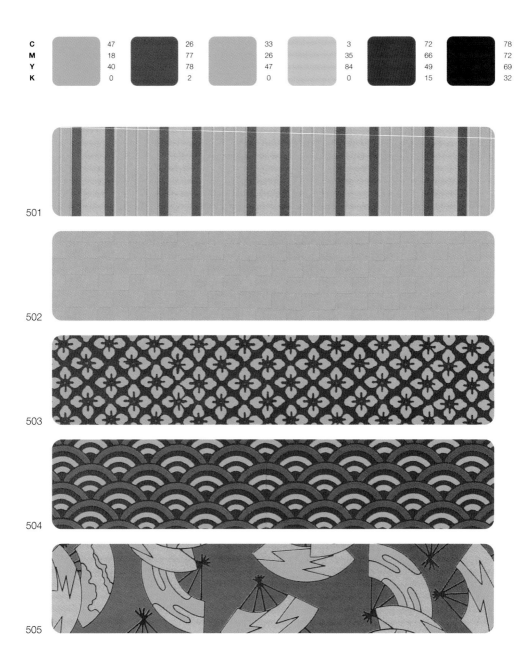

C		47		26		33		3		72		78
M		18		77		26		35		66		72
Y		40		78		47		84		49		69
K		0		2		0		0		15		32

501

502

503

504

505

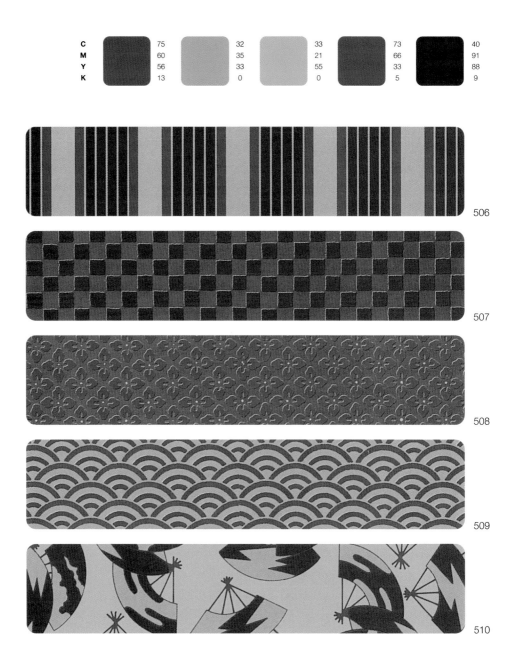

C	75	32	33	73	40
M	60	35	21	66	91
Y	56	33	55	33	88
K	13	0	0	5	9

506

507

508

509

510

C	79		27		31		57		47
M	62		1		15		20		61
Y	58		4		29		41		79
K	15		0		0		0		0

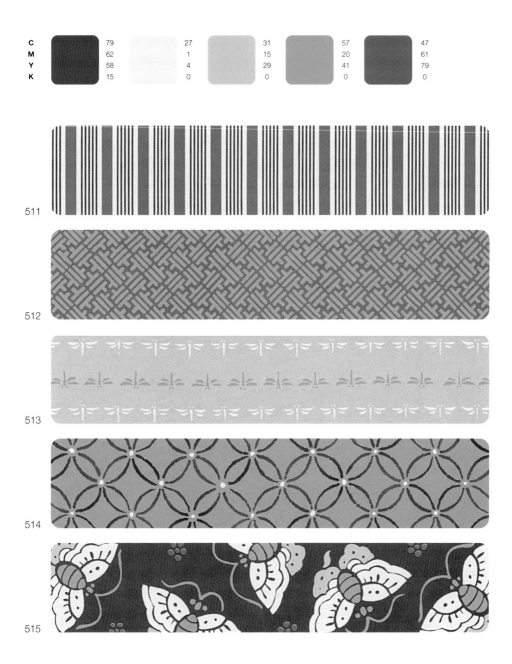

511

512

513

514

515

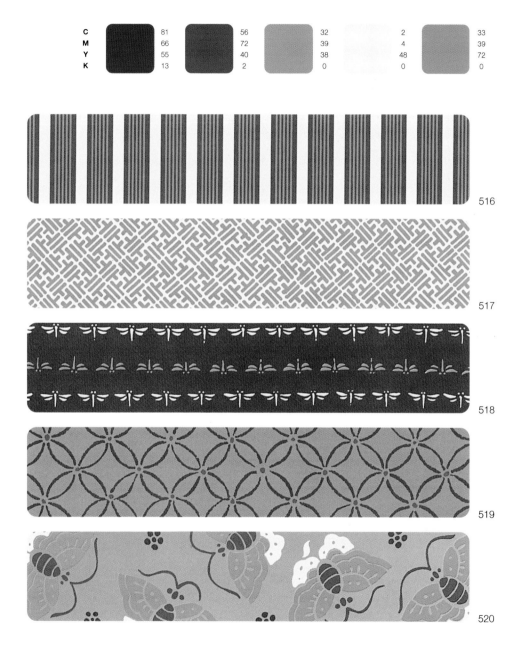

C	81	56	32	2	33
M	66	72	39	4	39
Y	55	40	38	48	72
K	13	2	0	0	0

516

517

518

519

520

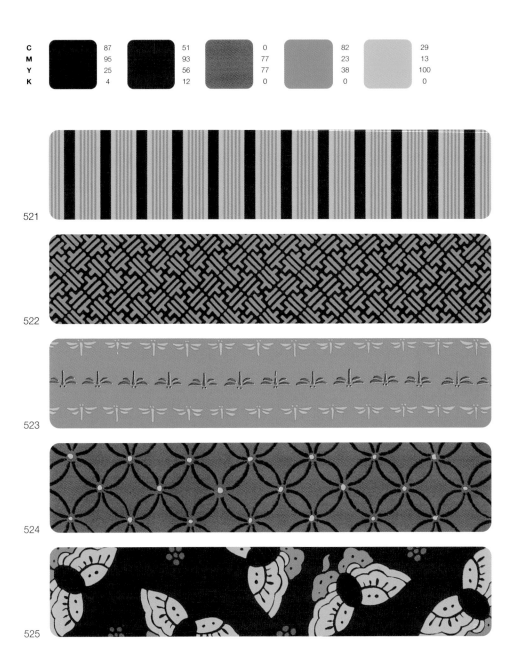

C	87	51	0	82	29
M	95	93	77	23	13
Y	25	56	77	38	100
K	4	12	0	0	0

521

522

523

524

525

C	84	50	0	23	52
M	91	21	24	23	75
Y	37	48	53	6	85
K	6	0	0	0	7

526

527

528

529

530

C	72	0	67
M	58	52	24
Y	47	87	55
K	4	0	0

27	51	
97	20	
38	8	
1	0	

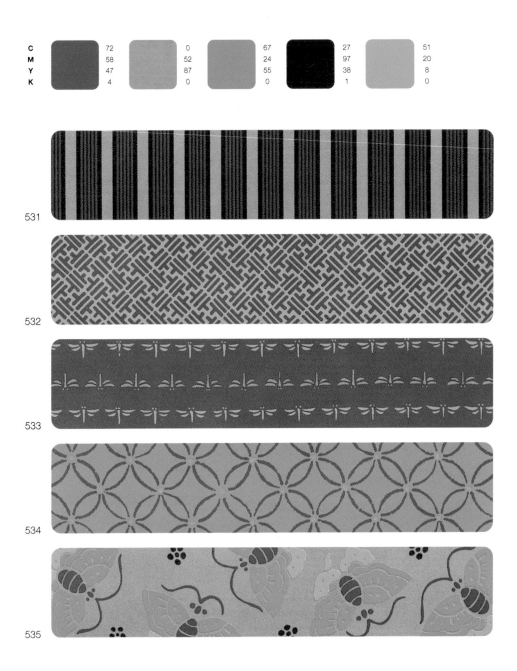

531

532

533

534

535

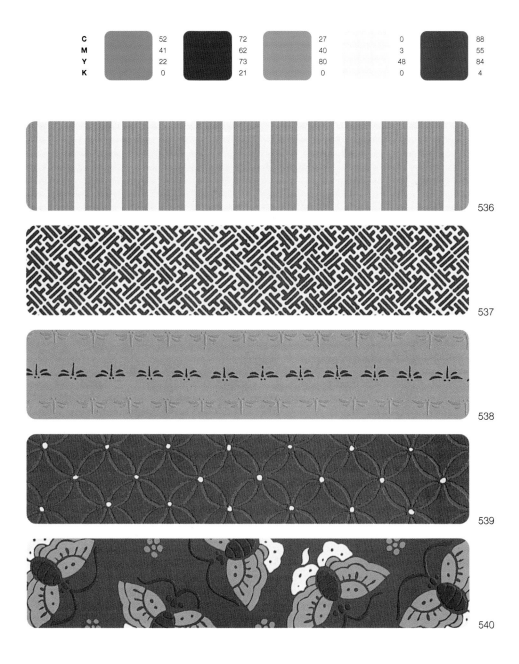

C	52		72		27		0		88
M	41		62		40		3		55
Y	22		73		80		48		84
K	0		21		0		0		4

536

537

538

539

540

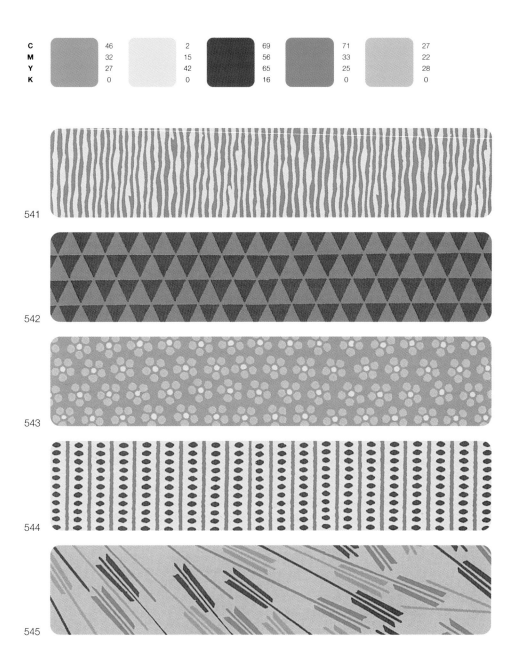

C	46	2	69	71	27
M	32	15	56	33	22
Y	27	42	65	25	28
K	0	0	16	0	0

541

542

543

544

545

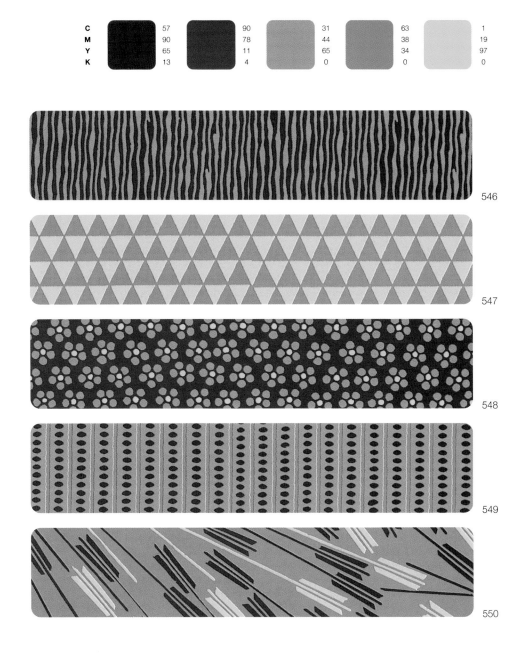

C	57		90		31		63		1
M	90		78		44		38		19
Y	65		11		65		34		97
K	13		4		0		0		0

546

547

548

549

550

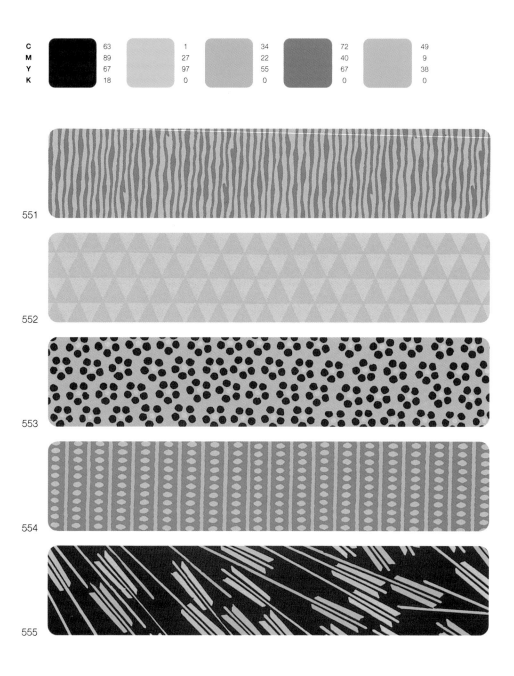

C	63		1		34		72		49
M	89		27		22		40		9
Y	67		97		55		67		38
K	18		0		0		0		0

551

552

553

554

555

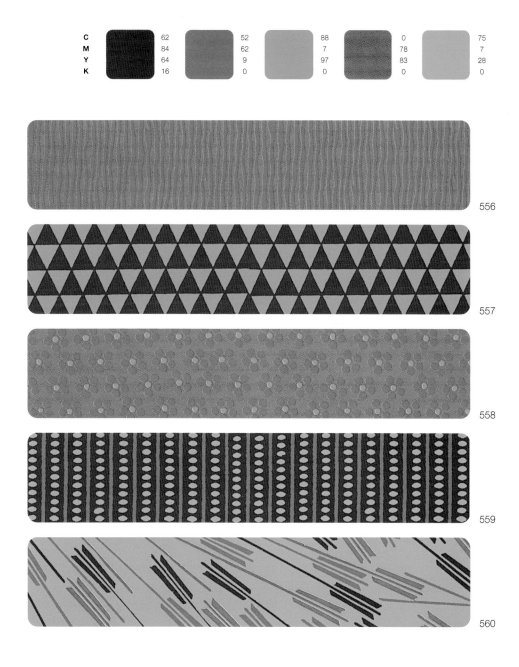

C	62		52		88		0		75
M	84		62		7		78		7
Y	64		9		97		83		28
K	16		0		0		0		0

556

557

558

559

560

C		28		23		22		52		86
M		91		7		23		53		50
Y		93		90		29		11		41
K		7		0		0		0		1

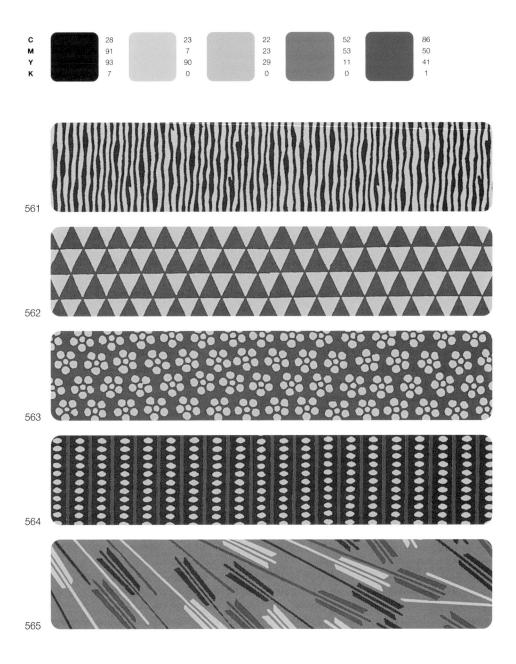

561

562

563

564

565

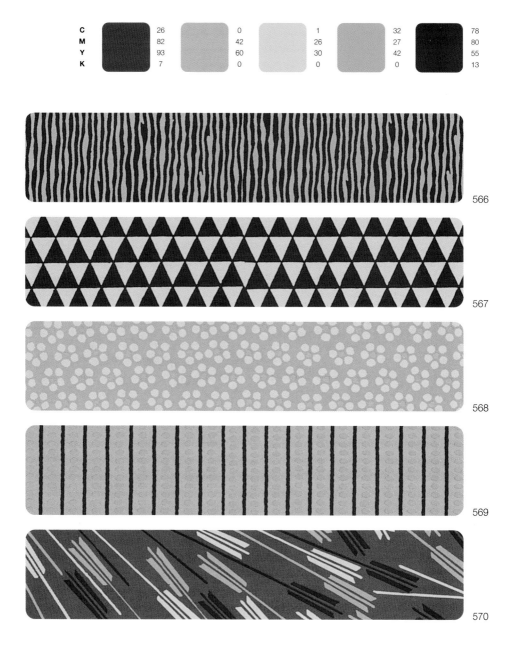

C		26		0		1		32		78
M		82		42		26		27		80
Y		93		60		30		42		55
K		7		0		0		0		13

566

567

568

569

570

C	27		1		0		35		71
M	81		28		9		4		71
Y	95		96		25		26		26
K	3		0		0		0		3

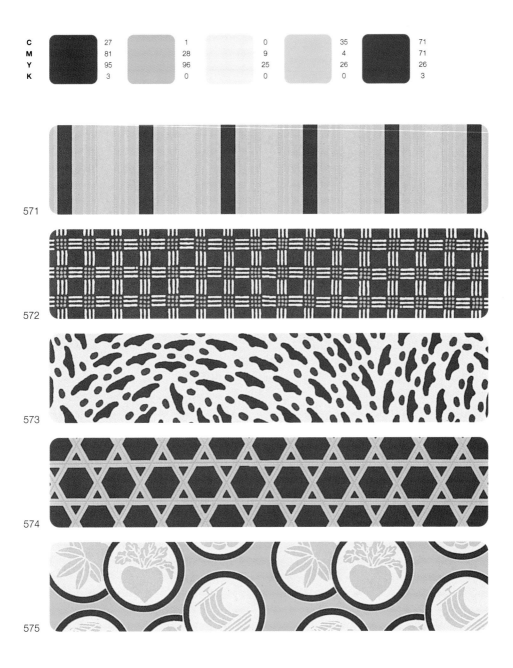

571

572

573

574

575

C		0		55		15		47		0
M		97		16		21		93		0
Y		82		21		97		61		0
K		9		0		0		10		100

576

577

578

579

580

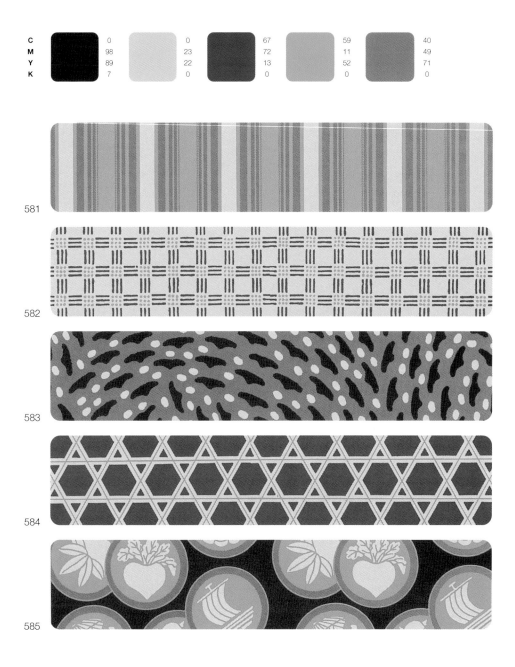

C	0	0	67	59	40
M	98	23	72	11	49
Y	89	22	13	52	71
K	7	0	0	0	0

581

582

583

584

585

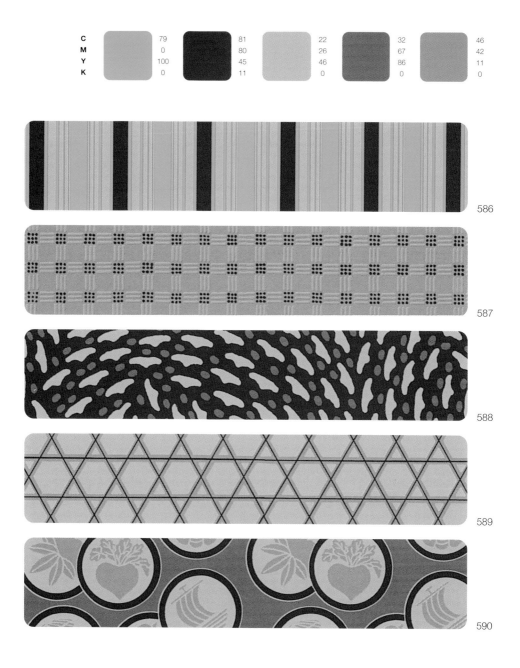

C		79		81		22		32		46
M		0		80		26		67		42
Y		100		45		46		86		11
K		0		11		0		0		0

586

587

588

589

590

C	81		0		71		52		1
M	0		29		61		54		29
Y	95		24		38		8		71
K	0		0		4		0		0

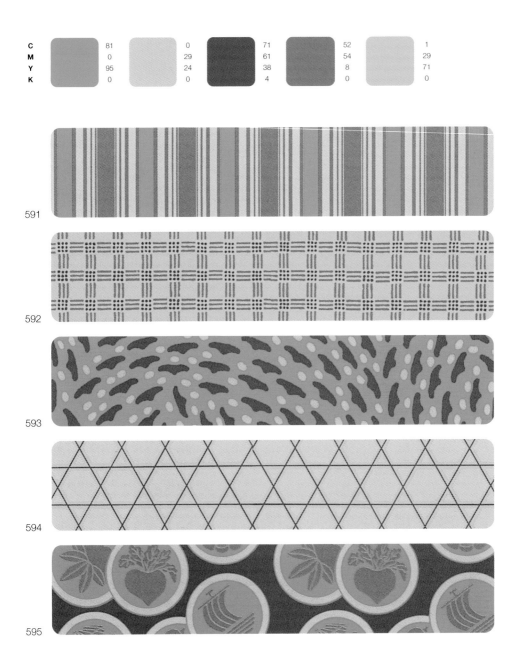

591

592

593

594

595

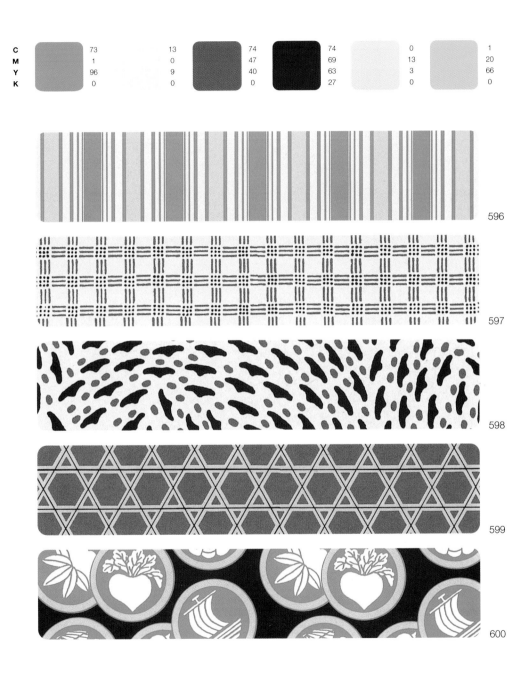

C	73		13		74		74		0		1
M	1		0		47		69		13		20
Y	96		9		40		63		3		66
K	0		0		0		27		0		0

596

597

598

599

600

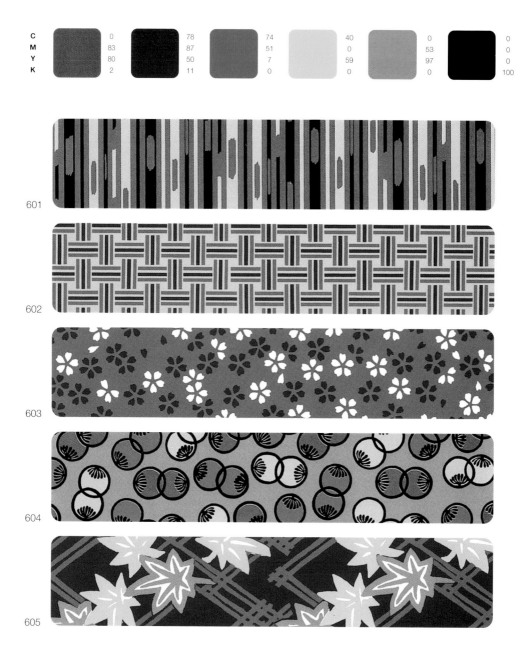

C	0		78		74		40		0		0
M	83		87		51		0		53		0
Y	80		50		7		59		97		0
K	2		11		0		0		0		100

601

602

603

604

605

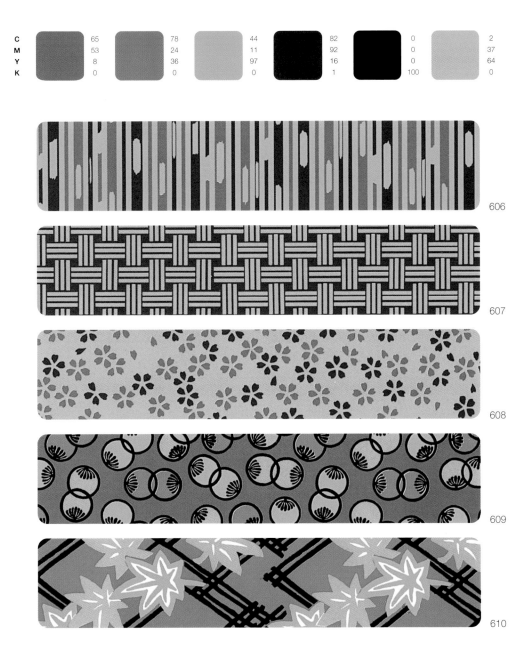

C	65		78		44		82		0		2
M	53		24		11		92		0		37
Y	8		36		97		16		0		64
K	0		0		0		1		100		0

606

607

608

609

610

C		64		72		21		25		44
M		47		69		32		72		5
Y		7		69		84		78		40
K		0		30		0		1		0

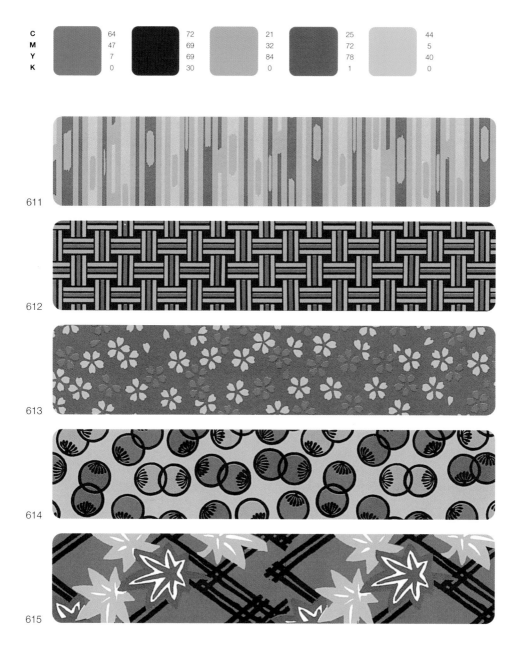

611

612

613

614

615

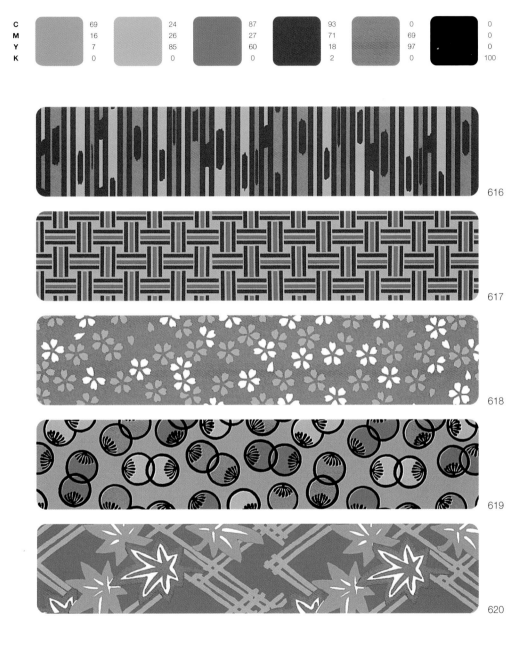

C	69	24	87	93	0	0
M	16	26	27	71	69	0
Y	7	85	60	18	97	0
K	0	0	0	2	0	100

616

617

618

619

620

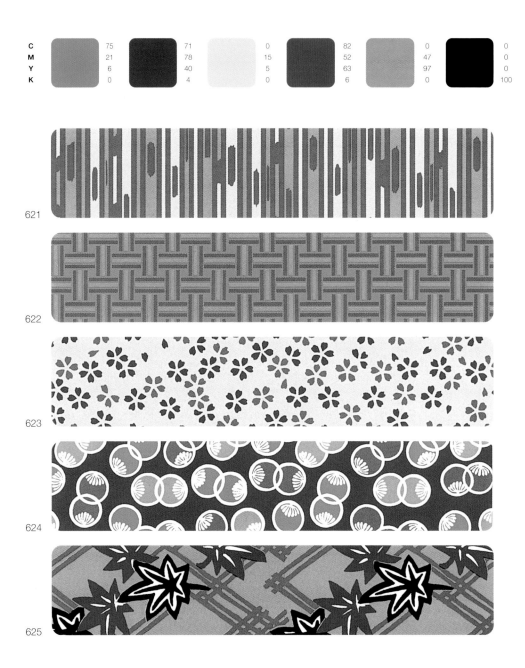

C	75		71		0		82		0		0
M	21		78		15		52		47		0
Y	6		40		5		63		97		0
K	0		4		0		6		0		100

621

622

623

624

625

C		75		0		58		33		15
M		24		0		95		38		11
Y		4		0		71		51		42
K		0		100		17		0		0

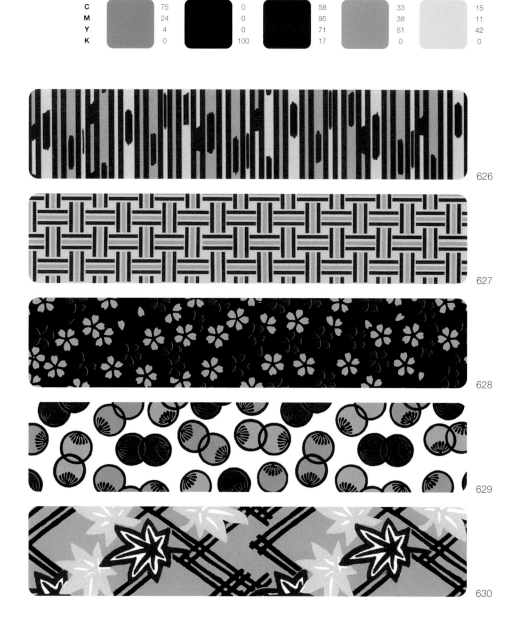

626

627

628

629

630

C		0		40		70		0		65
M		25		60		43		0		67
Y		97		78		95		0		7
K		0		0		0		100		0

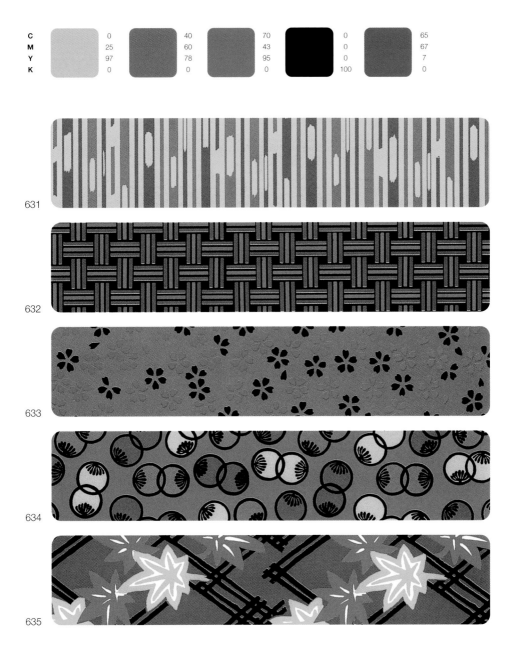

631

632

633

634

635

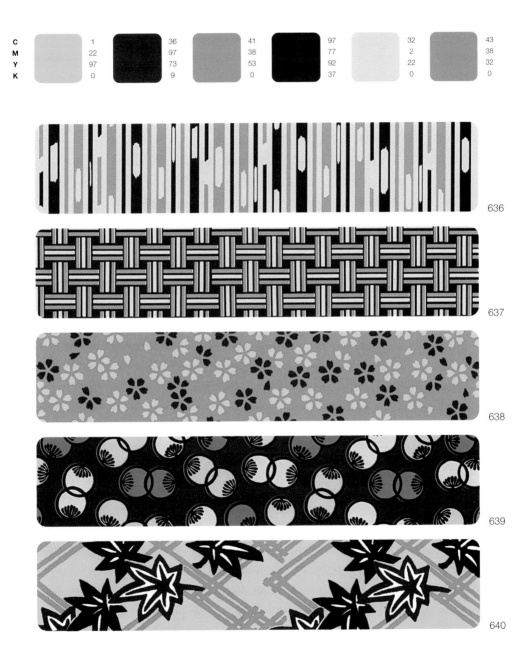

C	1		36		41		97		32		43
M	22		97		38		77		2		38
Y	97		73		53		92		22		32
K	0		9		0		37		0		0

636

637

638

639

640

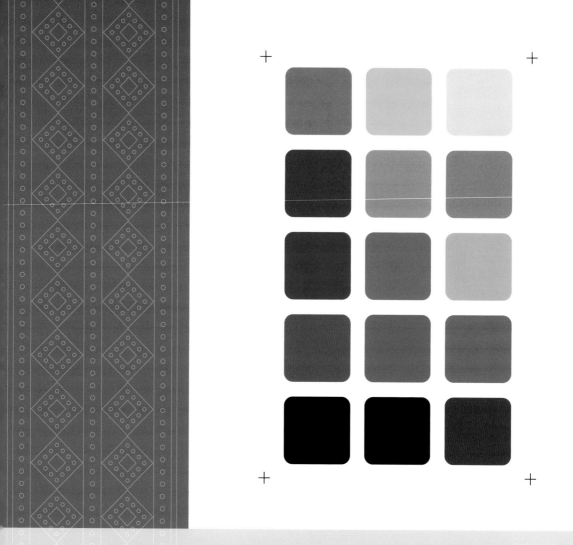

These colors are derived from natural dyes used in textiles and other raw materials. The understated tones blend well with this collection of worldly, tribal patterns and can be used to design a natural and restful environment with ethnic flair.

Natural

*Note: The color palette above is only a sampling of the color range Natural provides. See the following section for a broader selection of Natural colors.

C	85	0	28	0	67
M	32	79	44	0	81
Y	42	80	97	0	35
K	0	0	0	100	0

641

642

643

644

645

C	95		46		78		94		31
M	32		42		52		84		85
Y	47		40		84		44		55
K	0		0		1		14		4

646

647

648

649

650

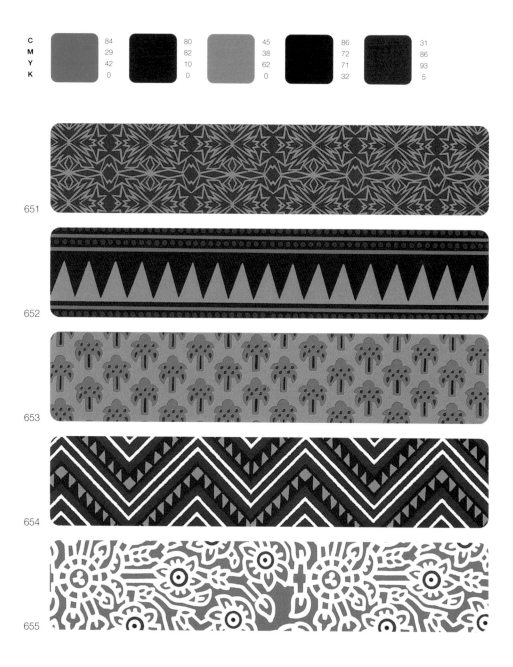

C	84		80		45		86		31
M	29		82		38		72		86
Y	42		10		62		71		93
K	0		0		0		32		5

651

652

653

654

655

C	81		37		60		82		93
M	69		44		88		10		94
Y	74		68		60		52		60
K	28		0		14		0		25

656

657

658

659

660

C		72		72		24		35		82
M		66		28		97		89		93
Y		71		63		35		85		80
K		21		0		0		9		41

661

662

663

664

665

C	76		35		48		73		73
M	68		64		40		74		97
Y	75		83		72		35		66
K	26		0		0		5		26

666

667

668

669

670

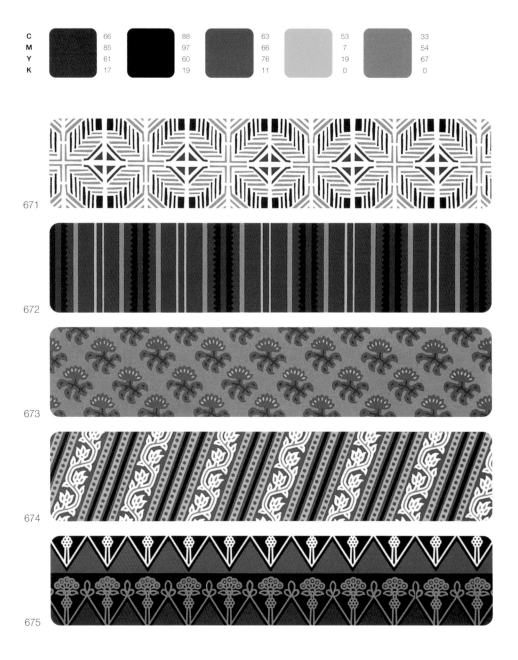

C	66		88		63		53		33
M	85		97		66		7		54
Y	61		60		76		19		67
K	17		19		11		0		0

671

672

673

674

675

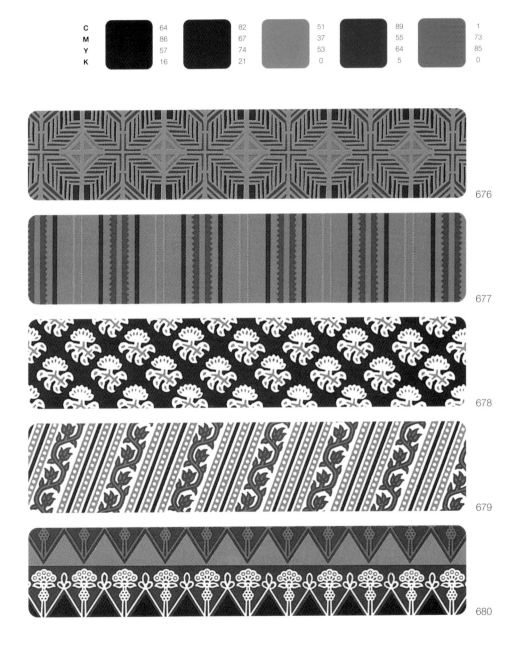

C	64	82	51	89	1
M	86	67	37	55	73
Y	57	74	53	64	85
K	16	21	0	5	0

676

677

678

679

680

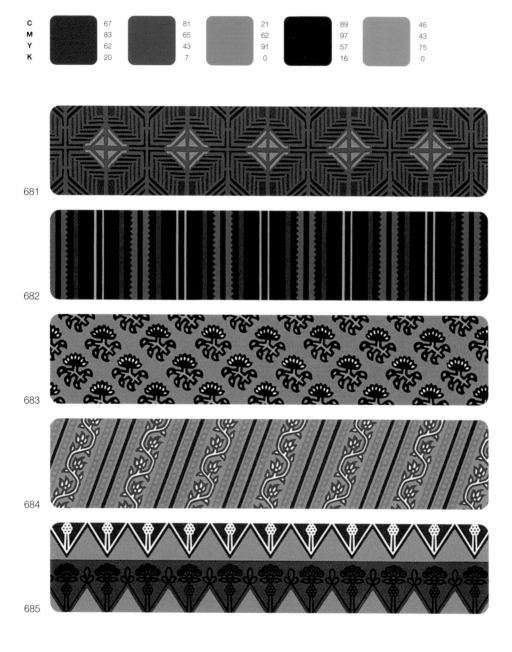

C	67	81	21	89	46
M	83	65	62	97	43
Y	62	43	91	57	75
K	20	7	0	16	0

681

682

683

684

685

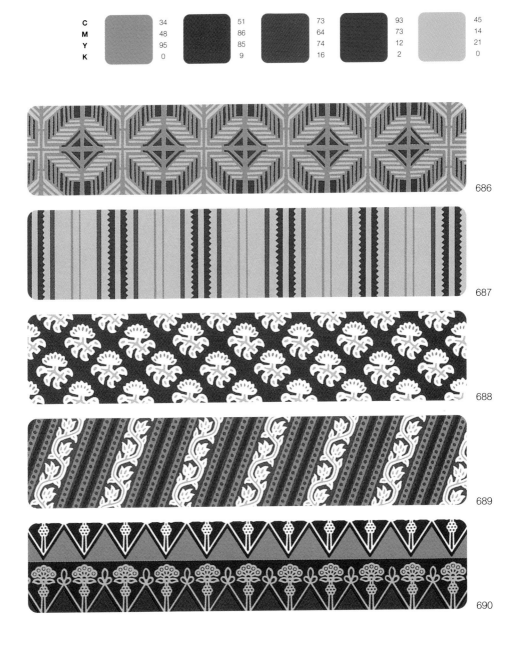

C	34		51		73		93		45
M	48		86		64		73		14
Y	95		85		74		12		21
K	0		9		16		2		0

686

687

688

689

690

C	36		0		54		94		85
M	47		0		23		35		78
Y	93		0		55		34		26
K	0		100		0		0		7

691

692

693

694

695

C		30		72		68		21		97
M		42		63		96		67		67
Y		86		58		67		25		60
K		0		21		26		0		15

696

697

698

699

700

C 76	83	53	0	85
M 45	89	40	82	67
Y 79	93	58	98	53
K 0	54	0	1	20

701

702

703

704

705

C	90	67	73	97	34
M	76	82	55	17	48
Y	80	69	54	97	81
K	24	12	2	0	0

706

707

708

709

710

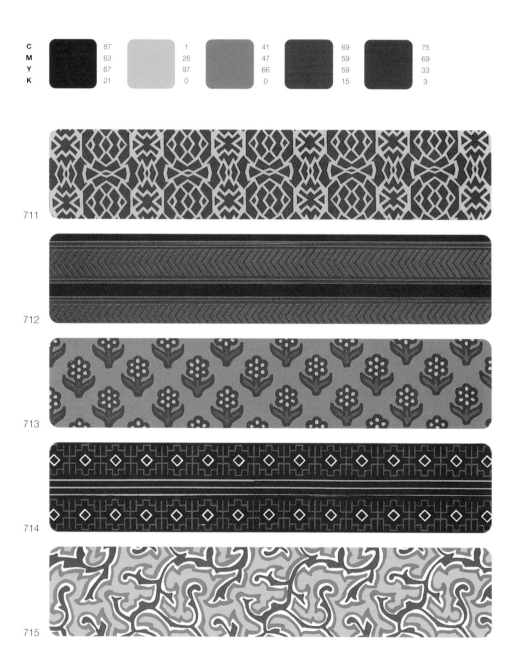

C	87		1		41		69		75
M	63		26		47		59		69
Y	67		97		66		59		33
K	21		0		0		15		3

711

712

713

714

715

C	81	60	33	42	42
M	66	38	40	68	18
Y	88	37	34	77	30
K	2	0	0	2	0

716

717

718

719

720

C		63		84		64		37		9
M		57		40		95		48		15
Y		79		66		68		96		64
K		9		1		22		1		0

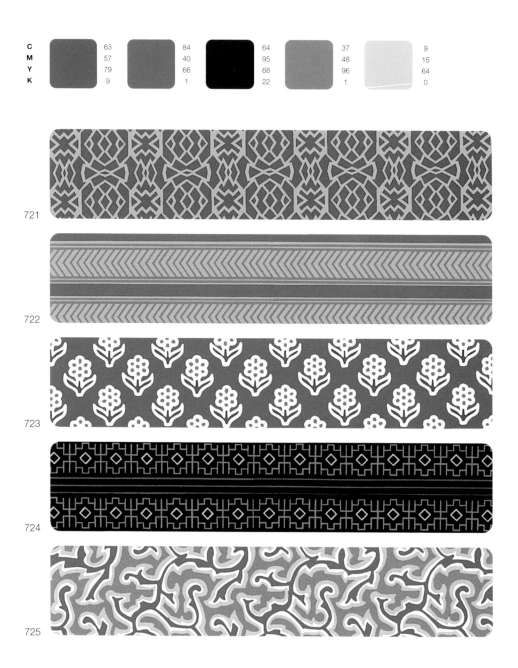

721

722

723

724

725

C	74		38		97		36		65
M	58		81		78		37		58
Y	83		84		42		55		25
K	1		6		7		0		0

726

727

728

729

730

C		31		56		56		0		76
M		72		52		52		52		51
Y		60		58		57		69		49
K		4		4		11		0		4

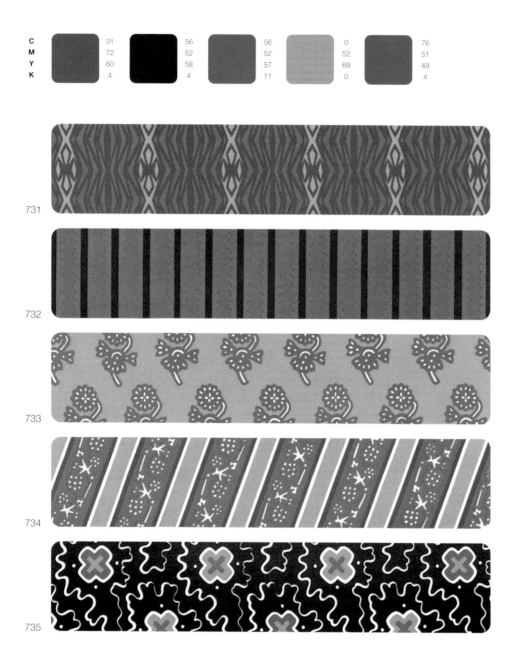

731

732

733

734

735

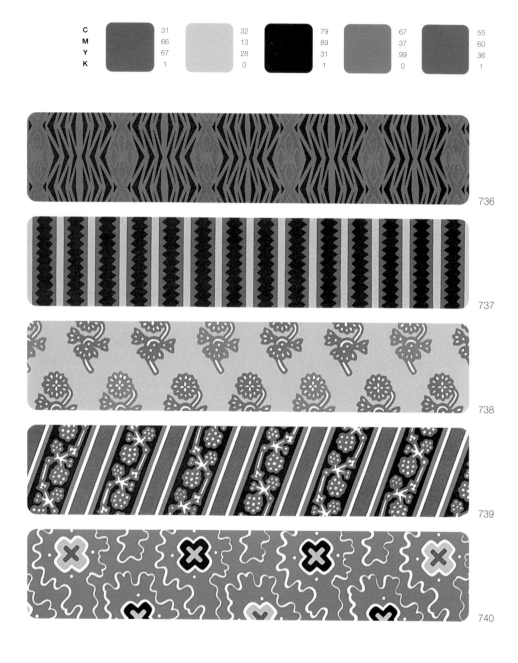

C	31		32		79		67		55
M	66		13		89		37		60
Y	67		28		31		99		36
K	1		0		1		0		1

736

737

738

739

740

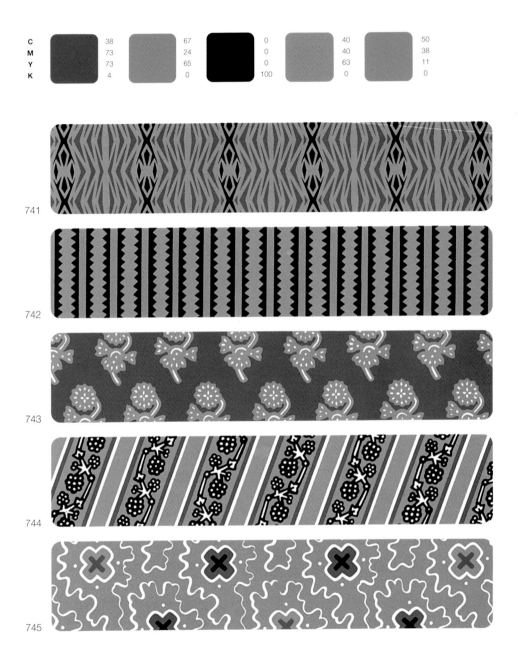

C	38		67		0		40		50
M	73		24		0		40		38
Y	73		65		0		63		11
K	4		0		100		0		0

741

742

743

744

745

C	69	16	38	37	66
M	57	23	97	18	64
Y	51	85	93	34	37
K	11	0	11	0	2

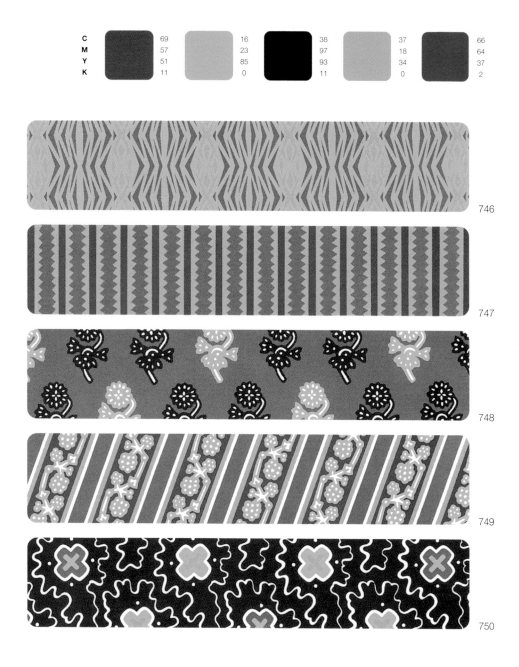

746

747

748

749

750

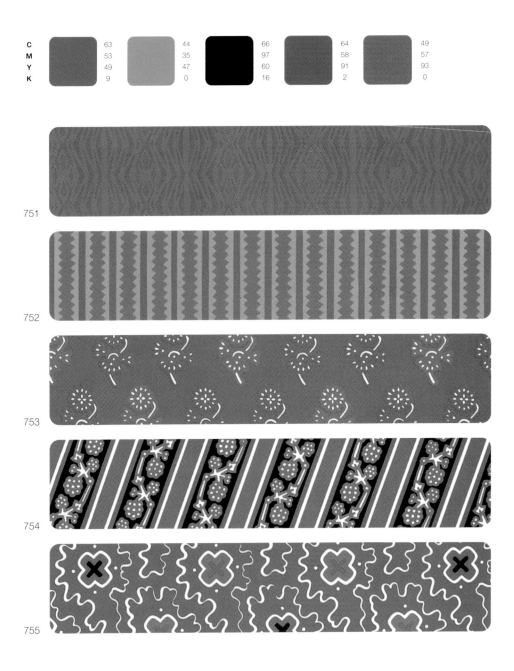

C		63		44		66		64		49
M		53		35		97		58		57
Y		49		47		60		91		93
K		9		0		16		2		0

751

752

753

754

755

C	77		13		2		58		59
M	64		26		71		50		44
Y	64		50		88		56		88
K	22		0		0		7		0

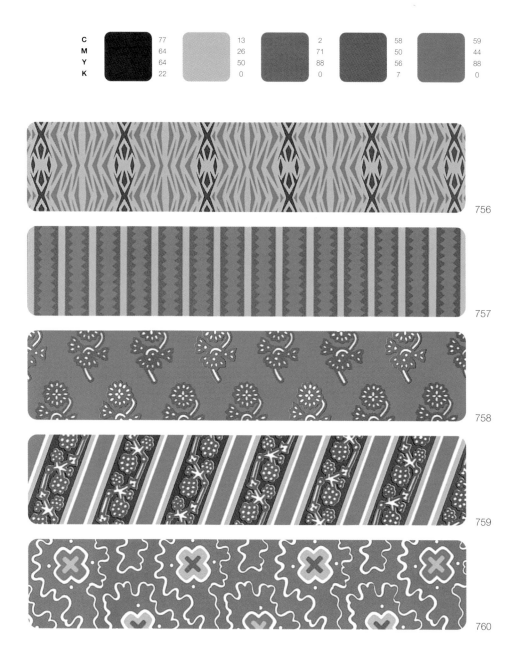

756

757

758

759

760

C 62	C 53	C 94	C 43	C 84
M 56	M 88	M 51	M 39	M 71
Y 82	Y 67	Y 71	Y 52	Y 76
K 6	K 13	K 2	K 0	K 35

761

762

763

764

765

C		0		29		27		15		68
M		0		45		76		10		94
Y		0		88		87		40		74
K		100		0		0		0		35

766

767

768

769

770

C		24		42		71		53		79
M		49		81		44		66		64
Y		96		75		100		83		71
K		0		9		0		5		18

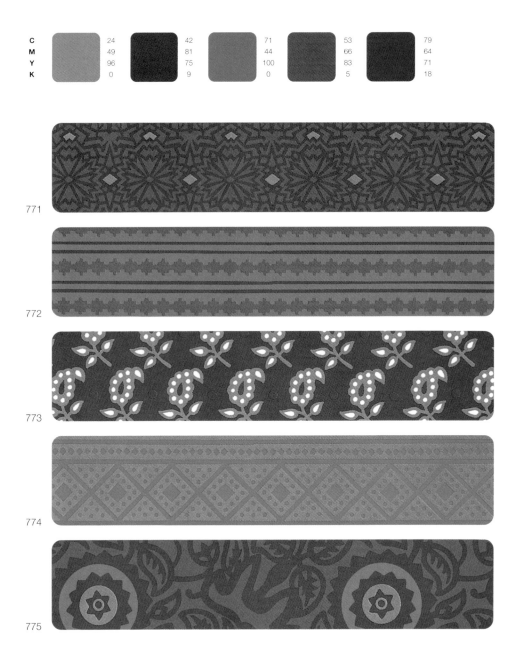

771

772

773

774

775

C		0		74		89		68		18
M		0		69		26		56		65
Y		0		30		60		50		95
K		100		5		0		13		0

776

777

778

779

780

C		0		93		67		76		53
M		0		63		77		70		40
Y		0		35		64		69		75
K		100		4		20		29		0

781

782

783

784

785

C	0	58	25	69	24
M	0	86	84	47	46
Y	0	58	76	49	97
K	100	11	5	1	0

786

787

788

789

790

C	47		68		87		31		89
M	89		68		8		40		65
Y	68		79		28		59		74
K	11		11		0		0		13

791

792

793

794

795

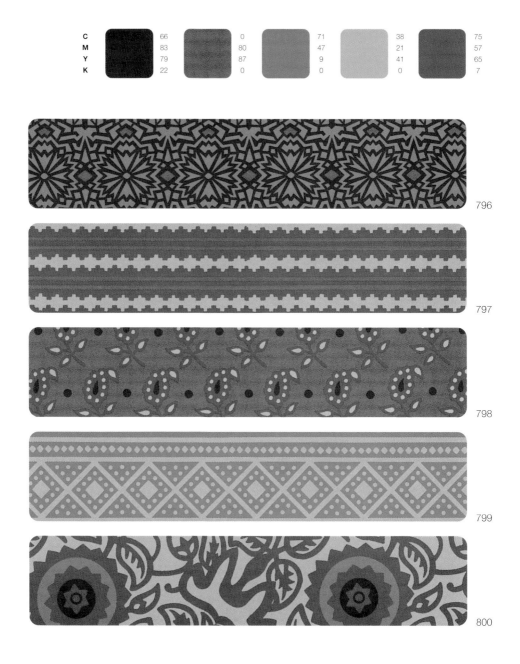

C	66		0		71		38		75
M	83		80		47		21		57
Y	79		87		9		41		65
K	22		0		0		0		7

796

797

798

799

800

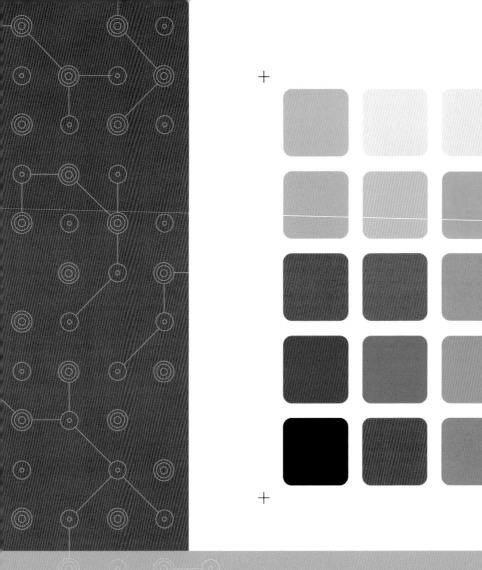

This palette is a mix of cool and muted hues drawn from metals and other building materials. Combining these colors with geometric and linear patterns produces a clean, high-tech look that can be used in a variety of applications.

Industrial

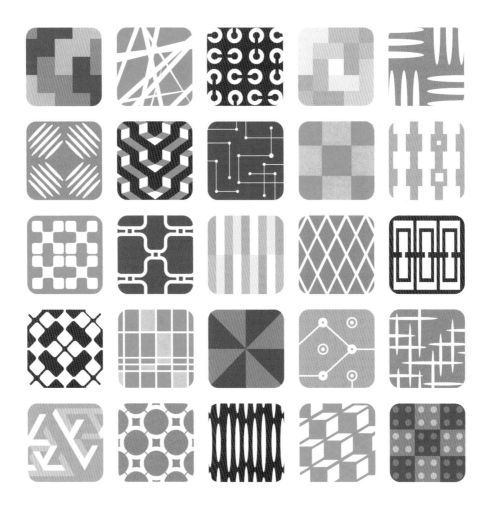

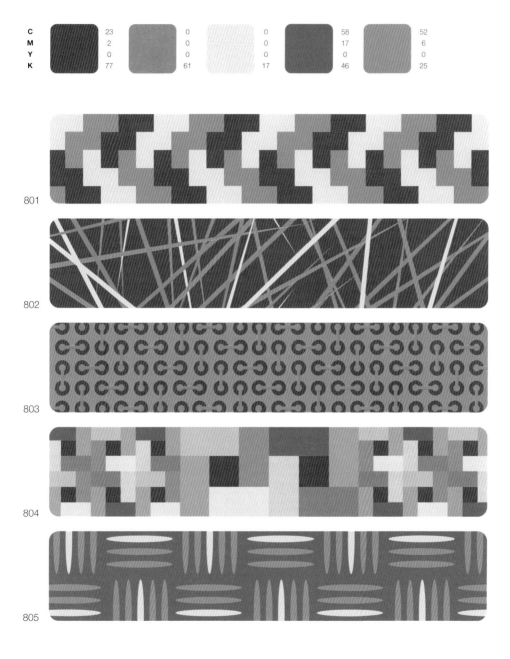

C	23		0		0		58		52
M	2		0		0		17		6
Y	0		0		0		0		0
K	77		61		17		46		25

801

802

803

804

805

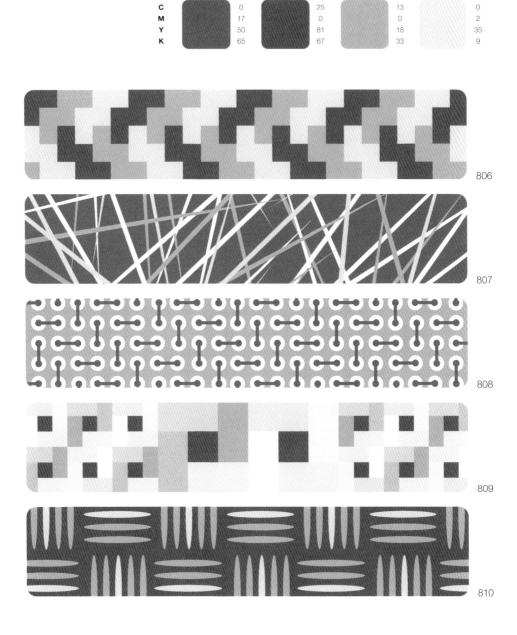

C	0		25		13		0
M	17		0		0		2
Y	50		81		18		35
K	65		67		33		9

806

807

808

809

810

C	0	25	58	0	0	0
M	13	0	17	0	0	0
Y	15	40	0	0	0	0
K	45	15	46	100	61	17

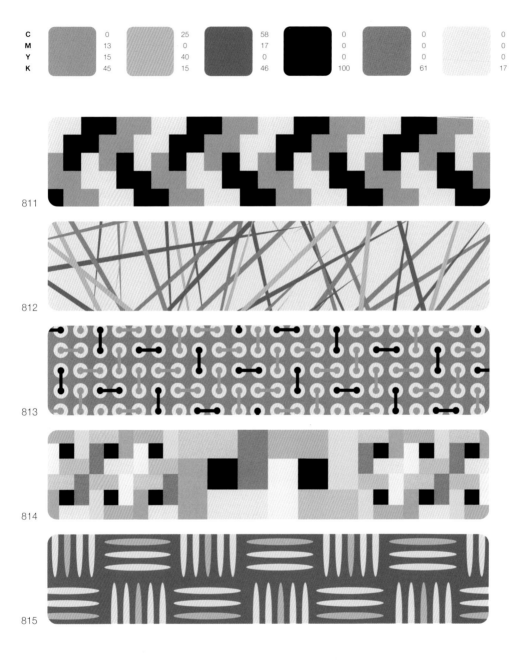

811

812

813

814

815

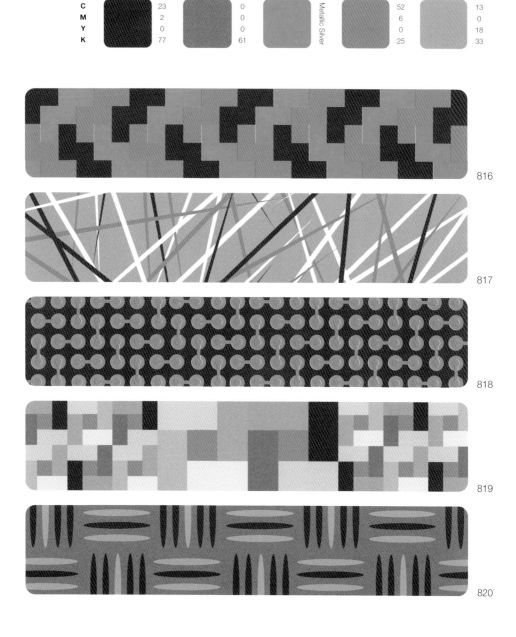

C										
C		23		0		Metallic Silver		52		13
M		2		0				6		0
Y		0		0				0		18
K		77		61				25		33

816

817

818

819

820

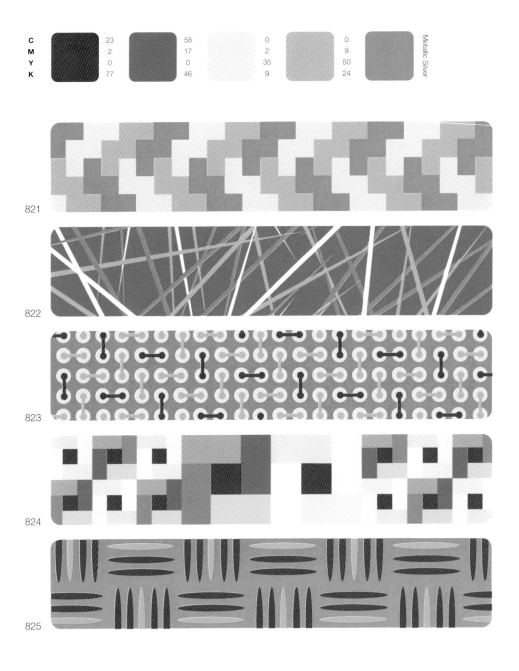

C	23	58	0	0	
M	2	17	2	9	Metallic Silver
Y	0	0	35	50	
K	77	46	9	24	

821

822

823

824

825

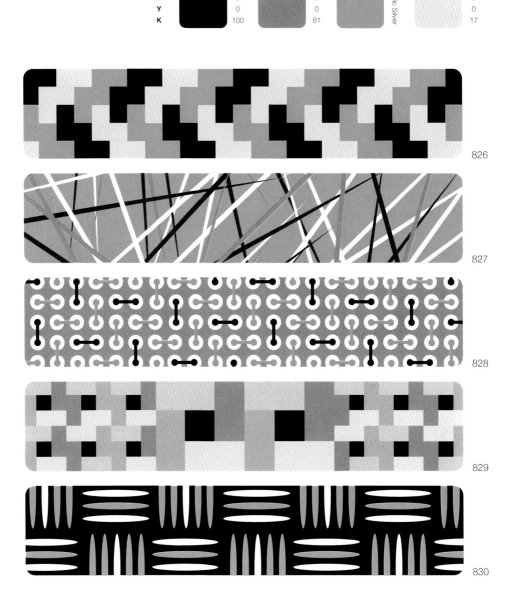

								Metallic Silver		
C		0		0		0			0	
M		0		0		0			0	
Y		0		0		0			0	
K		100		61		0			17	

826

827

828

829

830

C	80		13		0		0		0
M	0		0		2		0		0
Y	10		18		35		0		0
K	68		33		9		61		17

831

832

833

834

835

C	0		25		25		23		0		0
M	17		0		0		2		13		0
Y	50		40		81		0		15		0
K	65		15		67		77		45		17

836

837

838

839

840

C		58		52		13		
M		17		6		0		Metallic Silver
Y		0		0		18		
K		46		25		33		

841

842

843

844

845

C	0	25	52	0	
M	17	0	6	9	
Y	50	40	0	50	
K	65	15	25	24	Metallic Silver

846

847

848

849

850

C	0		0		80		25		52
M	0		13		0		0		6
Y	0		15		10		40		0
K	100		45		68		15		25

851

852

853

854

855

C	23	0	Metallic Silver	52	13	0
M	2	0		6	0	9
Y	0	0		0	18	50
K	77	61		25	33	24

856

857

858

859

860

C		0		0		80		0		25		52
M		2		13		0		17		0		6
Y		35		15		10		50		81		0
K		9		45		68		65		67		25

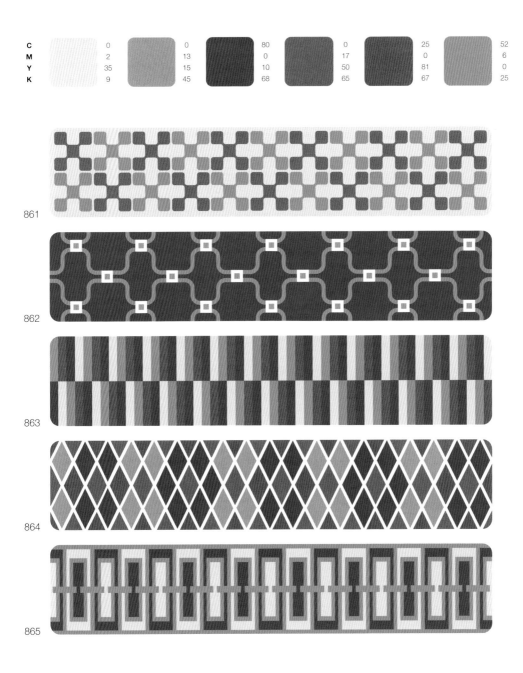

861

862

863

864

865

Pattern and Palette Sourcebook

C	0	25	25	58	0
M	17	0	0	17	9
Y	50	81	40	0	50
K	65	67	15	46	24

866

867

868

869

870

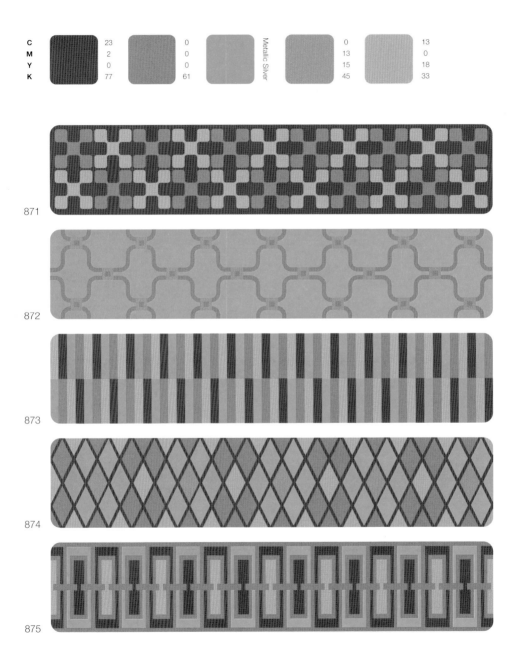

C	23		0		0	Metallic Silver	0		13
M	2		0		0		13		0
Y	0		0		0		15		18
K	77		61				45		33

871

872

873

874

875

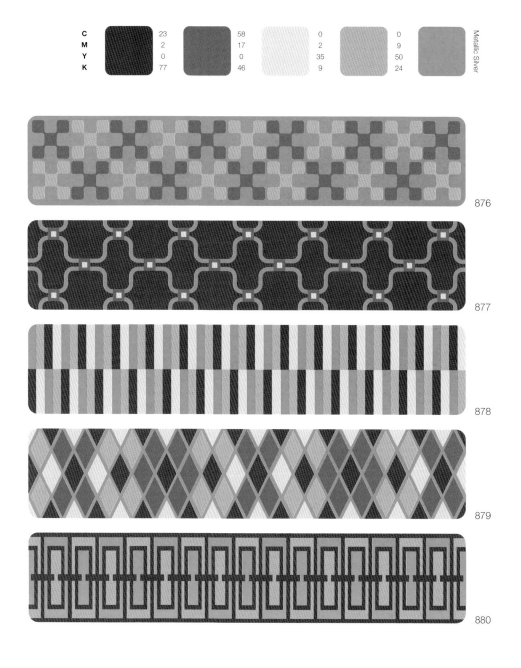

C		23		58		0		0		Metallic Silver
M		2		17		2		9		
Y		0		0		35		50		
K		77		46		9		24		

876

877

878

879

880

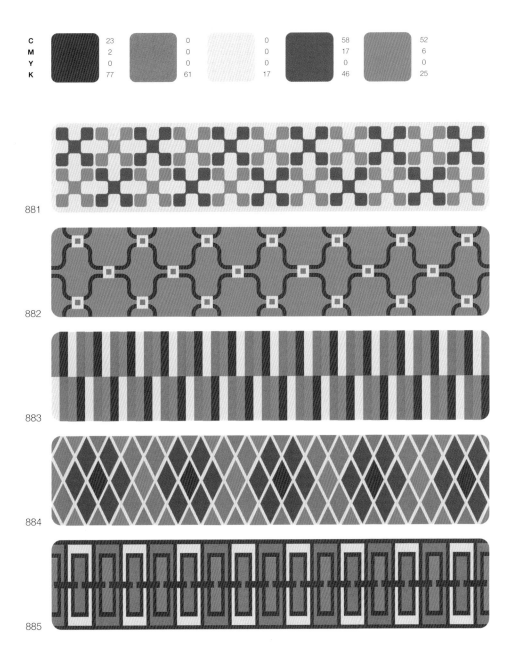

C	23		0		0		58		52
M	2		0		0		17		6
Y	0		0		0		0		0
K	77		61		17		46		25

881

882

883

884

885

C	0	0	80	25	52
M	0	0	0	0	6
Y	0	0	10	40	0
K	100	17	68	15	25

886

887

888

889

890

C	0	0	0	80	0
M	17	9	2	0	0
Y	50	50	35	10	0
K	65	24	9	68	100

891

892

893

894

895

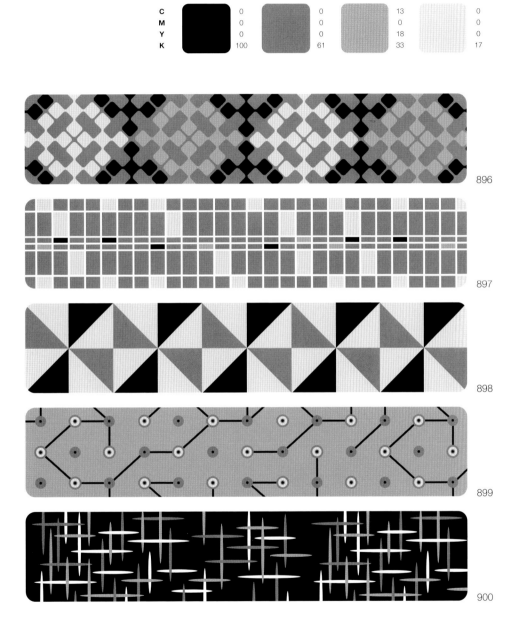

C		0		0		13		0
M		0		0		0		0
Y		0		0		18		0
K		100		61		33		17

896

897

898

899

900

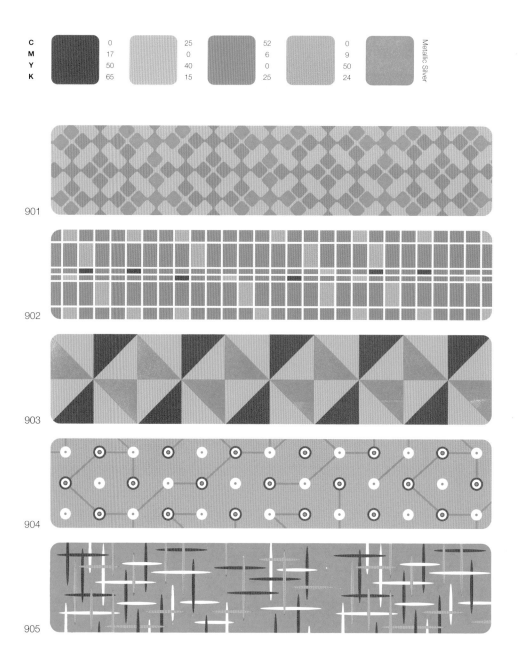

C		0		25		52		0		
M		17		0		6		9		
Y		50		40		0		50		Metallic Silver
K		65		15		25		24		

901

902

903

904

905

C	0		0		80		0		25		52
M	2		13		0		17		0		6
Y	35		15		10		50		81		0
K	9		45		68		65		67		25

906

907

908

909

910

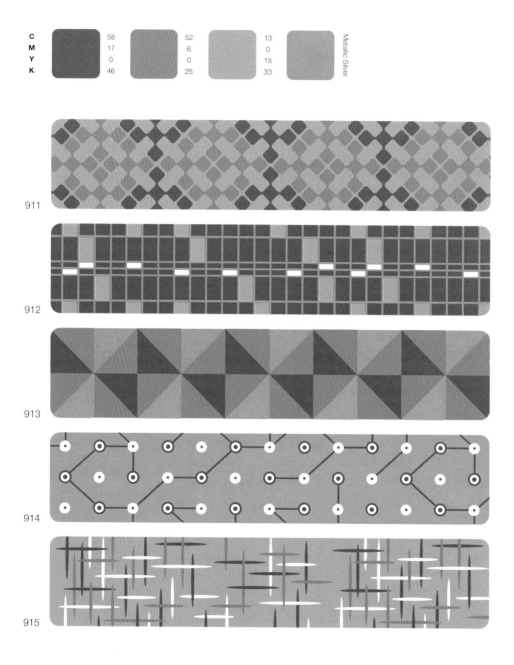

C	58	52	13	
M	17	6	0	
Y	0	0	18	Metallic Silver
K	46	25	33	

911

912

913

914

915

C	0		25		25		23		0		0
M	17		0		0		2		13		0
Y	50		40		81		0		15		0
K	65		15		67		77		45		17

916

917

918

919

920

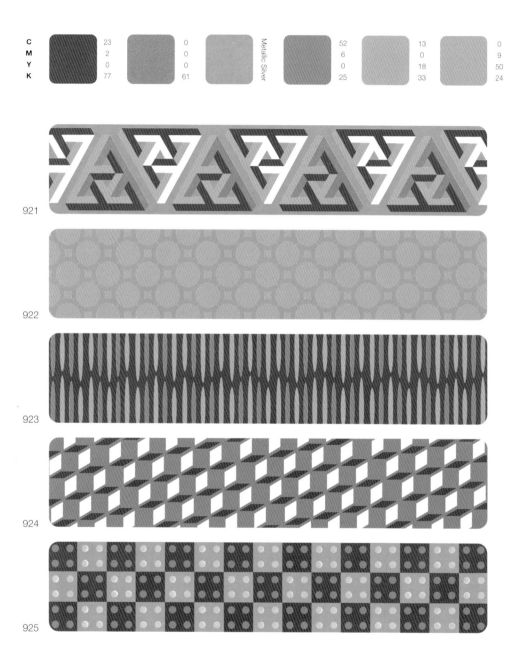

C	23		0			Metallic Silver	52		13		0
M	2		0				6		0		9
Y	0		0				0		18		50
K	77		61				25		33		24

921

922

923

924

925

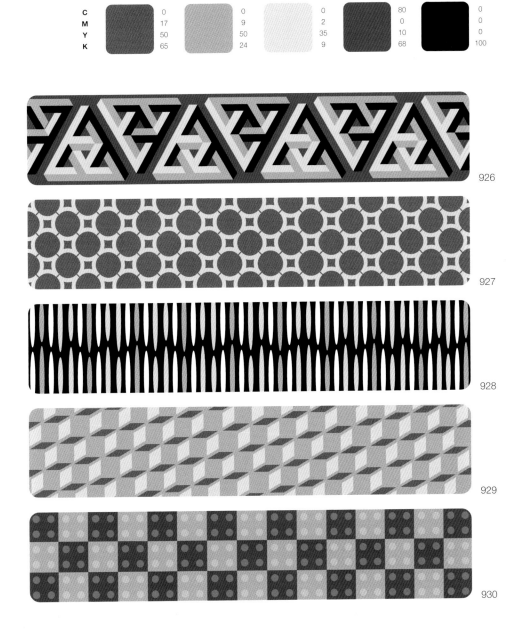

C 0 0 0 80 0
M 17 9 2 0 0
Y 50 50 35 10 0
K 65 24 9 68 100

926

927

928

929

930

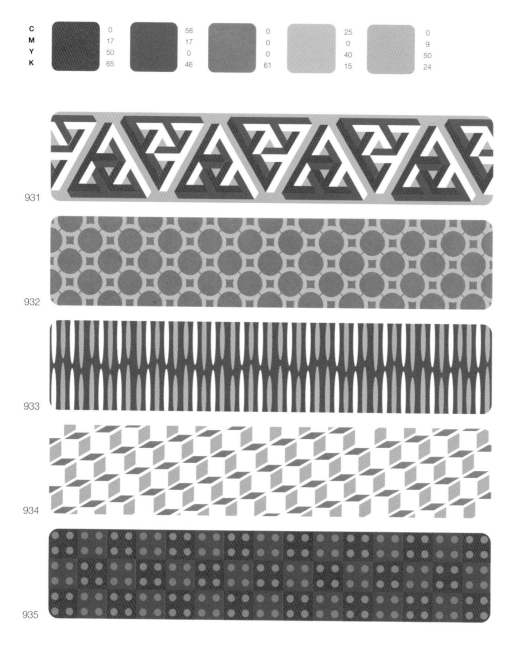

C		0		58		0		25		0
M		17		17		0		0		9
Y		50		0		0		40		50
K		65		46		61		15		24

931

932

933

934

935

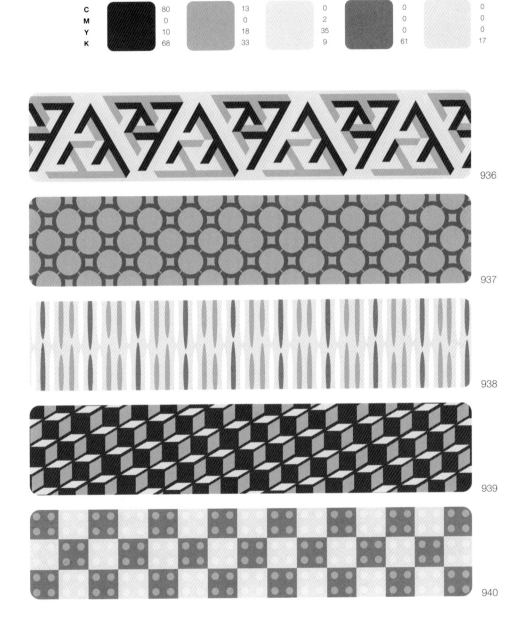

C	80	13	0	0	0
M	0	0	2	0	0
Y	10	18	35	0	0
K	68	33	9	61	17

936

937

938

939

940

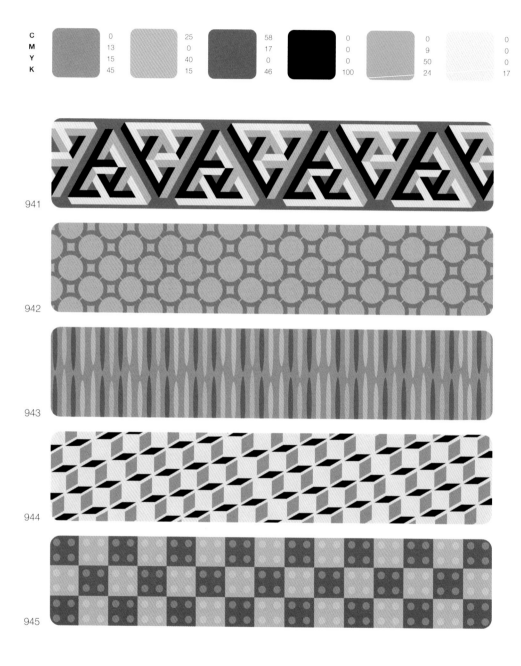

C		0		25		58		0		0		0
M		13		0		17		0		9		0
Y		15		40		0		0		50		0
K		45		15		46		100		24		17

941

942

943

944

945

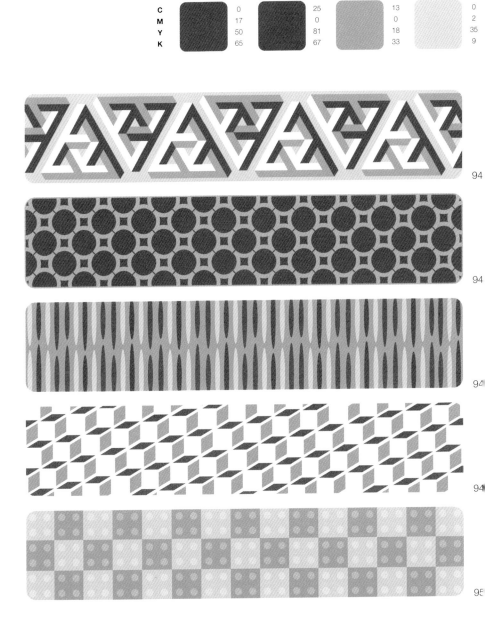

C	0		25		13		0
M	17		0		0		2
Y	50		81		18		35
K	65		67		33		9

94

94

94

94

95

About the Author

Anvil Graphic Design, Inc.

Anvil is a graphic design and branding consultancy based in Redwood City, California, that began extensive experimentation with patterns in 1999. They had sensed a need for well-designed gift wrap and decided to shake things up by mixing traditional Asian motifs with a twist of modernism. The outcome was an annual selection of gift wrap that was given away as a holiday promotion to clients, business associates, and friends. After receiving an unprecedented number of accolades within the design industry they decided to mass produce the paper and sell it wholesale. Thus, their second business, Anvil Modern Paperie was born.